PRACTICAL

SUFISM

PRACTICAL
SUFISM

A GUIDE TO THE
SPIRITUAL PATH

Based on the Teachings of Pir Vilayat Inayat Khan

PHILLIP GOWINS

QUEST
BOOKS

Theosophical Publishing House
Wheaton, Illinois * Chennai, India

Copyright © 2010 by Phillip Gowins
First Quest Edition 2010

Quest Books
Theosophical Publishing House
P. O. Box 270
Wheaton, IL 60187-0270
www.questbooks.net

Cover design by Beth Hansen-Winter
Typesetting by Wordstop Technologies, Chennai, India

The author wishes to thank the Sufi Order International for permission to
quote from the works of Hazrat Inayat Khan and Pir Vilayat Khan.

Library of Congress Cataloging-in-Publication Data

Gowins, Phillip.
Practical sufism: a guide to the spiritual path based on the teachings of
Pir Vilayat Khan / Phillip Gowins.—1st Quest ed.
    p.   cm.
Includes bibliographical references and index.
ISBN 978-0-8356-0881-7
1. Sufism.   2. Inayat Khan, Pir Vilayat.   I. Title.
BP189.6G69 2010
297.4—dc22   2010017980

5 4 3 2 1 * 10 11 12 13 14

Printed in the United States of America

To the memory of Pir Vilayat Inayat Khan, my teacher and my friend

Riding on the horse of hope,
Holding in my hand the rein of courage,
Clad in the armor of patience,
And the helmet of endurance on my head,
I started on my journey to the land of love.
—Hazrat Inayat Khan

CONTENTS

FOREWORD

Sufis tend to emphasize that, as a form of communication, words are too limited to have great value. Even Rumi, the prolific poet, whose thirty thousand verses top American best-seller lists 750 years after his death, scoffed at the ability of words to convey "that Reality." A Sufi book, then, is something of a paradox. It is a collection of words about something that cannot be conveyed in words. Phillip Gowins, in this insightful personal narrative, acknowledges as much, more than once.

Why read it, then? Rumi, asked a similar question, replied, "Words set you searching. They are not the objects of your quest. . . . Words are like glimpsing movement far in the distance. You start in that direction to see better." And so, in reading the words that follow, you set your feet on a trail.

Just the act of picking up this book and glancing at it suggests that you are a seeker. You may have been intrigued by its title and wanted to know more. You may even have heard about Sufis and wondered who they are.

Like so much else encountered on the Sufi Path, the word *Sufi* itself is mysterious in its origin and manifold in its meanings. Some are convinced that the word has its origins in the Arabic term for the coarse woolen cloaks that early seekers wore; others insist that it comes from the Arabic word for the verandas where those closest to Muhammad fervently prayed. Another derivation suggests a common ancestry with the Greek *sophia*, or wisdom. Many prefer to look to *saaf*, or purity, to explain the name. For Sufis, however, such debates are of only mild interest. It is being that captivates their attention.

The automatic and unthinking response of many scholars is to categorize Sufis as Islamic mystics. Like many "definitions" connected with the Sufi Path, this one has elements of truth, yet is not completely true. For many centuries, Sufis—or, as they are alternately known, dervishes—have found the warmest welcome in countries and areas that have embraced Islam, as a quick glance at the names of Sufi teachers and saints demonstrates. While many Sufis are devout, observant, and orthodox Muslims, however, many others are less orthodox, and many others are adherents of other religions. Sufis frequently point out that, although the name *Sufi* is associated with the followers of the Prophet Muhammad, spiritual seekers known by other names both predated him and greeted him once he arrived. The Sufi Way is not a religion or a component of a religion but the heart of all religions and spiritualities. So far is it from dogma that Sufi teachers often express their discomfort with the term *Sufism*, which suggests a rigid and fixed doctrine.

It is also very common for Sufi teachers to spend considerable time and energy explaining other things that the Sufi Path is *not*. In different ways, the masters all emphasize that Sufis offer no one-size-fits-all philosophy, no shalt and shalt-not commandments, no guarantees, and no clearly delineated goal. As *Practical Sufism* demonstrates, progress on the path demands a constellation of qualities—commitment, authenticity, patience, surrender, love, and yearning, among others—but the evocation and balance of these characteristics are unique for each individual.

Because there is no equivalent of a catechism or a creed for Sufis, teachers are essential. The very presence of a teacher helps a student progress spiritually, and much teaching is transmitted nonverbally. Because teachers are channels for divine light, initiates of Sufi orders preserve knowledge of the *silsila*, or chain of transmission from one teacher to the next. The silsila can be likened to an electrical cord that carries the charge from the source of power to a particular lamp. Because Sufis adapt to conditions and populations that vary and change, however, there are many groups, or orders, of Sufis. Orders have originated in many locales and are found all over the world. Each order has its own personality and flavor, coming as it does from a particular place and the interpretations of individual teachers. Just as each lamp in a house can appear different and shed light in its own way, though, each order draws on the one source of power acknowledged by all Sufis: Divine Love. A Sufi may be affiliated with the Naqshbandi Order, or the Ni'amatullah, Mevlevi, Qadiri, Rifa'i, Bektashi, Tijani, Shadhili, or one of many others. The distinctions among Sufis are considered much more significant than their similarities.

The author of the present book is part of the Sufi Order International, a Chishti branch of the Sufi Path. The silsila of this order, like those of all genuine Sufi orders, begins with the Divine One, followed by the Angel Jibra'il, or Gabriel, and then the Prophet Muhammad and the blessed Ali. It proceeds to a thirteenth-century Syrian saint who initiated Afghanis in the Sufi Way and from there to a series of saints who migrated to Gujarat, India, and taught there for hundreds of years.

In 1910, an initiate of this order, under instructions from his own spiritual teacher, brought the Sufi Message to the West. Hazrat Inayat Khan thus began a great spiritual awakening and transformation of those who heard him speak and read his writings. In the span of only seventeen years, Pir-o-Murshid (Leader and Teacher) Hazrat (Holy Presence) Inayat Khan begin the Sufi Movement in North America and Europe. A gifted and celebrated master of Indian classical music, he sacrificed his composing and performing to teach tolerance, love, unity, and consciousness. Upon his early death, his son Pir Vilayat Inayat Khan succeeded him. In 2000, Hazrat Inayat Khan's grandson, Pir Zia Inayat Khan, assumed leadership of the Sufi Order. These are the teachers of whom Phillip Gowins writes. His many years of close communion with Pir Vilayat and his decades of teaching and leadership enable him to write from experience and first-hand knowledge about *tasawwuf,* the Sufi Path.

The way in which he writes is identifiably Sufi. Like Rumi's *Masnavi* and Sa'adi's *Gulistan* (and many other Sufi works), this book appears to have very little pattern. On the surface, it seems to be a fascinating tangle of anecdotes, autobiography, philosophy, practices, references, reflections, musings, and meanderings. A casual reader might find the organization oddly elastic, or even suspect that there is very little organization at all.

The casual reader would be mistaken. As Sufis constantly remind us, there is a lot going on below, above, and beyond the surface. There is a jazzy rhythm to this writing that echoes the unpredictable syncopation of life itself. Our attention seems to be drawn first here, to a memory of a guide, then here, to a recollection of a student's frustrations, then there to something Pir Vilayat said on retreat. In trying to follow the apparent digressions and circular stories, we may feel that we are losing our concentration, our grip on what we are being told. We may become anxious about whether we are getting the point.

And that, of course, is precisely the point—that we can let go and surrender to a pattern that we may not easily discern, that we can give up control and linear logic and just immerse ourselves in what is given. Phillip Gowins invites us along for a ride and tells us that we do not need to drive the car, that we can admire the scenery and enjoy the journey. Like the very best storytellers, he keeps us so spellbound that we do not worry about the bumps in the road and the bends in the tale. It may be some time before we even notice that, though he sits in the driver's seat, his hands seldom grip the wheel. There is a pattern in this book—but it is not imposed by either reader or writer. It emerges.

As you begin the wonderful trip through these pages, though, you do not really need to map out where you are going. It is needless to worry about patterns or fret about what exactly a Sufi is. Just glimpse the movement far in the distance, as Rumi suggested. Let the words set you searching.

Debra Bunch Ghosh (Abi-Ru Shirzan)
November 2005

Acknowledgments

Some fifteen years ago, I had picked up my teacher, Pir Vilayat Inayat Khan, at the airport and was taking him into New York City. We were chatting about nothing much, as we often did, when he suddenly turned to me and said, almost commanded, "Write a book!"

I distinctly remember turning to look at him in disbelief, thinking he was pushing his luck asking me to write a book. After all, books on Sufism are written by scholars or by men and women at his level. But, a few years later, acting on an inner impulse that I am sure he planted, I wrote my first tentative paragraphs and slowly began to compose.

As the book grew, it seemed to take on a life of its own, and I was its helpless but willing servant—an emotion I know is shared by many other writers and artists. I do not think I was really compelled, as Pir Vilayat was a great believer in free will. Besides his apparent and surprising trust in me to do something useful, I do know that I would never have completed the book were it not for a few very special people.

First and foremost is my adored wife, Majida Dawn Gowins, who continually kept telling me to keep on writing and who put up with my typing on the computer at 5:00 a.m. Then there is my beloved friend Zumurrud Butta, whose constant encouragement and support made me believe that I just might have something to say. Then there are the people who read through first drafts and gave me the feedback that I needed to keep

going: my stepdaughter, Uriel Belinda Gray; my friends Siddiqi
Heather Ferraro and Roshan Jennifer Ferraro; Muhasaba Molly
Wender; and Gabrielle Weeks. Lastly comes John Chambers,
who believed in the book and published the first edition.

*The lower self is like a thief who sneaks into your house at night
to steal whatever is valuable and worthwhile. You cannot fight
this thief directly, because it will mirror whatever force you bring
against it. If you have a gun, the thief will also have a gun. If
you have a knife, the thief will have a knife as well. To struggle
with the thief is to invite disaster. So, what can you do?*

*The only practical solution is to turn on the light.
The thief, who is a coward at heart, will then run out.
How do we turn on the light? Through the practice of
remembrance, awareness, and heedfulness.*

—Sheikh Tosun Bayrak

INTRODUCTION

One night when I was twenty-six, I was lying in bed next to my wife—my first wife, I mean—waiting to fall asleep, when a sensation like a traveling electric shock swept down through my body.

I thought nothing of it until it happened again. It happened a third time, then kept on happening at three- or four-second intervals. It was like a pulsing hoop of energy that started at my head and coursed down through my entire body—like a wave front hitting the beach again and again. I was puzzled, then alarmed, then frightened, then really scared, until I was begging it to stop. But it just went on and on. It seemed to be happening on some psychic level, maybe in my aura (though I did not know what an aura was then), and despite my pleading I remember thinking that it was really all right, that no actual harm was being done to me. Just when I thought it was over, another wave came crashing down, exploding, enlivening, energizing me. Then it stopped. I lay there for a long time, not daring to sleep for fear the energy would sneak up on me again. At the same time I was amazed, even pleased, that something unusual had happened to me, because nothing much had ever happened to me in my life before. But I was exhausted, and I soon fell asleep. My wife, lying beside me, had not stirred.

When I got up the next morning I went into the bathroom to look at myself in the mirror for some sign of change—a pentagram carved into my forehead, perhaps, or a white streak running down the middle of my hair—some sign I had not just dreamed this shimmering wave of energy that kept me awake and affected me in some unknown but possibly profound way. But I saw nothing, no outward sign, only the same old lazy, frightened loser who looked back at me from the mirror every day, the same old frustrated failure who was well on his way to joining the league of disappointed, unpleasant old men who sit in badly lit taverns in cities all over the world telling each other lies about their adventurous youth. The phenomenon did not repeat itself the next night, and it never happened again. But I thought that if what had happened had really happened, then something had to have changed inside me, or in my life—hadn't it?

Later, I would come to view this experience as a wakeup call, my spiritual alarm clock going off.

For a long time I had strongly suspected that I was not a very interesting or likable person, certainly not one interesting enough to attract a bizarre unknown field of energy in the middle of the night. In those days I was mystified by life, clueless, adrift, frightened, insecure, and intelligent. I knew I was smart. I just did not know what at. College did not interest me. Not much interested me. I had a wife I did not know how to be with and a son I did not know what to do with. Later came a daughter, who further confused me. I did not know how to express affection or joy or any emotion at all except perhaps the disdain and contempt that come from the false pride people put on when what they really feel is unworthy. My opinions were as changeable as the wind, except for two things: I liked sex (that was a firm opinion), but I suspected I was not very good at it (a common enough guy terror, I suppose), and I had just discovered pot, which I thought was totally wonderful (remember, we are talking 1970 here). How I envied people who had firm convictions and expressed them unequivocally! Any authentic opinions I had about life and the world were so totally hidden within me as to be unknown even to myself.

The next stage in my (as yet to be revealed as such) spiritual odyssey took place when I was sitting in a state of reverie on the living room floor of our house in Oregon (I may have been stoned), gazing out the window at a very tall, very green pine tree. I was thinking that the world was a big objective whole unto itself and not just the series of disconnected perceptions we all have of it. This way of looking at things may be very familiar to some, but to me it was new at the time, and I was much enamored of it. It had also dawned on me that this objective whole might be a conscious, living entity—alive like myself—and that if I wanted to be of use to this world, then I should seriously dedicate myself to being a conscious, aware part of its single-entity aliveness. And then, suddenly, I took a vow to whatever cosmic forces rule that whatever I could do, or however those forces could make use of me so that I could be of service to the world, then I was at their disposal.

This was something that came from so deep inside me it surprised me. But I knew, truly knew, that I meant it. Whatever cosmic forces were listening must have taken me seriously, because a few months later my life completely fell apart, which I now know happened because I had triggered a crucial change in myself that demanded nothing less than the total dismantling of all the life I had lived before. What shape did this falling-apart take? My wife left me and took the children with her. There followed a series of misadventures, at the end of which I found myself on the other side of the United States in Boston, living in my brother's spare room. It had taken about two years for all this unpleasantness to unfold. As it did, I was constantly aware in the back of my mind that the vow I had made to the cosmos was the precipitating factor, and I could not help saying to myself that if this one simple vow could make so much happen, then what might I be able to accomplish if I could place a completely serene mind at the service of God?

I persisted in my confused and aimless state for another couple of years. From time to time, I leafed idly through a book or two on spirituality or meditation or an even more bizarre aspect of esoteric thought. Sometimes, I made attempts to meditate. I attended seminars, some of them given by people who certainly knew what they were talking about, though I was not prepared to accept that at the time. Then, one night, I looked into the mirror again, but this time it was the mirror of my soul. I had a third experience. There was nothing esoteric or paranormal about it. It was a humiliating sort of experience and one we all have from time to time. I had been reflecting on some concepts having to do with spirituality and thinking how clever I was to be able to understand the concepts I was reflecting on, when all of a sudden my thoughts coalesced into a single reproach directed at me. It was, "And just who do you think you are?" I did not like what I was seeing in my mind's eye. It was ugly. I saw self-pity and cowardice and just about every other negative quality attributable to man. I saw pettiness and a lack of sympathy. This was hardly calculated to make me feel good. But I also saw that I hardly even knew how to feel good.

I decided it was time for a beer. But I could not find one in the house. So I did the only other thing that I now realize was possible for me, personally, to do at the time. I took another vow, this time to change this personality of mine. I took a vow never to forget what I had seen in myself that night and to alter every aspect of it.

I did not go to a therapist. That is not a step I wanted, or would ever want, to take. Call it a personal quirk. Instead,

4

I began to develop the spiritual techniques that I still use to-day, techniques that work for me—and techniques that are not magical, that cannot be described glibly, and that consist of a lot of steady, plodding work.

To resume my narration: We are now in February 1979, and, as I have said, I was living in my brother's spare room in Boston. There I continued (what had now become) my spiritual search. It was not entirely spiritual. One of the things I was in search of was a girlfriend, and I found one. This girlfriend led me to my teacher.

One day we walked into a lecture room in the Sufi Center in midtown Boston to listen to a talk by Pir Vilayat Inayat Khan, spiritual head of the Sufi Order International. I caught my first glimpse of Pir Vilayat. And I knew that I had come home.

Pir Vilayat Inayat Khan was sixty-three at the time. I saw, seated before me on a raised dais, a short man with fierce black eyes, a carefully trimmed white beard, and a vigorous shock of hair brushed back neatly from his forehead. The description I give is an inadequate one—and it is mostly an irrelevant one, since it describes the physical Pir Vilayat. What I really picked up was a wave of energy—an oddly familiar wave of energy—that frightened the bejesus out of me and would continue to do so for quite some time.

That afternoon, Pir Vilayat spoke on the subject of meditation. I had never met anyone with so sharp a mind combined with so totally compassionate a being. I felt compelled to follow this person. Three months later I underwent *Bayat*, "the taking of hands"—the Sufi ceremony of commitment. Now I was a Sufi, since you do not "become" a Sufi but rather are a Sufi from the moment you commit yourself to the Order, with your Sufihood, which was always there, manifesting more and more as you advance along the path.

By the time I underwent Bayat, I had found out a great deal about my teacher. Pir Vilayat's father, Hazrat Inayat Khan, was born in India. His mother, Ora Ray Baker, was a cousin of Mary Baker Eddy, founder of the Christian Science movement in America. Hazrat Inayat Khan founded the Sufi Order in 1910, the Sufi Movement in 1916 in London, and finally the International Sufi Movement in Geneva, Switzerland, in 1922. He brought the movement to the United States shortly thereafter.

Pir Vilayat Inayat Khan was born in London in 1916. Shortly before his death in 1926, Hazrat Inayat Khan had named his son as his eventual successor. Pir Vilayat graduated from the Sorbonne at the University in Paris, France, in 1940, after completing studies in philosophy and psychology. He did postgraduate work at Oxford University and studied composition and cello at the École Normale de Musique in Paris.

Pir Vilayat Inayat Khan served as an officer in the British Royal Navy during World War II. He was assigned the duties of mine sweeping during the invasion at Normandy. His sister, Noor-un-Nisa Inayat Khan, served in the French Resistance as a radio operator. She was a vital link between the British War Office and the French underground, and her heroic services played a key role during the landing at Normandy. Minutes before she would have flown to safety, she was arrested by the Gestapo, imprisoned, escaped, and recaptured. She was finally taken to Dachau, where she was tortured and killed.

After the war, Pir Vilayat pursued his spiritual training with masters of different religious traditions throughout India and the Middle East. An acknowledged Pir in the lineage of the Chishti Sufi Order of India, he pursued an eclectic approach to spirituality that did not confine itself exclusively to Sufism, attempting to integrate the knowledge he had gained from his Western education with the overview, intuitions, and mastery developed during his spiritual training in Sufi, Hindu, Buddhist, Judeo-Christian, and Islamic traditions. On June 17, 2004, Pir Vilayat Inayat Khan, surrounded by his family, died peacefully at his home in Suresnes, a suburb of Paris. His son, Pir Zia Inayat Khan, had been the acting spiritual leader of the Sufi Order International since 2000. Pir Zia is also the founding director of the Suluk Academy, an esoteric school located in upstate New York. Pir Zia Inayat Khan's initiatory heritage integrates the transmissions of the Chishti, Suhrawardi, Qadiri, and Naqshbandi lineages within a post-denominational, interspiritual trajectory. He holds a master's degree in religion from Duke University.

Pir Vilayat has said the following about his work:

I am trying to develop an updated spirituality for our times. Following my father's message, I believe that to develop our being to its highest potential we need to discover our ideal and allow an inborn strength, a conviction in ourselves, to give us the courage toward developing this ideal. This requires both knowing our life purpose and mastery or discipline over ourselves in terms of body, mind, and emotions. With an attitude of joy and enthusiasm, we do not suppress but instead control and direct impulses toward the fulfillment of our goals. Instead of viewing life's setbacks as a hindrance, we can see them as an opportunity to discover and develop our creative power. As noted in all the religions, and most clearly evidenced in the life of Christ, we can transform suffering into joy. This means not denying suffering, but rather accepting it, and thus gaining strength to be more masterful in life. At this time I believe we are called upon to give up resentments and prejudices, no matter how difficult that may be. Individual resentment hinders our unfoldment toward becoming our highest ideal;

collective resentment causes wars. My deepest goal is to give those with whom I come into contact a respect and tolerance for each world religion, recognizing the unity of ideals behind the diversity of forms. I believe in rising above distinctions and differences to appreciate the beauty and variety in people and cultures and to uphold at all costs the dignity of every human being.

For twenty-seven years, almost every time Pir Vilayat Inayat Khan traveled from his home in France to the New York area, I heard him speak and attended his retreats; sometimes I served as his chauffeur and aide. But *Practical Sufism* is not an "official" text of the Sufi Order International, and in my book I am not proselytizing or trying to convert anyone to Sufism. For me, Sufism and the teachings of Pir Vilayat have served as a point of departure, a touchstone guiding me in the exploration of my inner being. Each person who desires to do so will find his or her own path. This is mine.

Throughout *Practical Sufism* I often quote the writings of Pir Vilayat Inayat Khan. Sometimes I quote the writings of his father, referring to that Sufi master as Pir-o-Murshid Hazrat Inayat Khan, the word *Pir* meaning "elder" and the title Pir-o-Murshid being reserved for those universally held in high esteem by the Sufi Order. Other times, I refer to Pir Hazrat Inayat Khan as simply Pir-o-Murshid or as Murshid.

Murshid means "teacher" and signifies the level of Self-realization usually applied to the head of an order. A "representative" is someone a pir or a murshid appoints to represent that pir or murshid to students to whom the teacher will not necessarily have time to attend properly. A "sheikh" is roughly the equivalent of a pir or murshid. But these definitions are not rigid, and different Sufi orders have different hierarchical breakdowns.

My wife—Majida—and I are representatives. Majida's Christian name is Dawn, but, like members of most esoteric orders, she was given a "spiritual" name by her teacher to differentiate her greater Self from her mundane personality; *Majida* means "The Glorious." I have a spiritual name too, *Musawwir*, which means "Artist" or "Fashioner." Majida and I are what is known in the spirituality business as field workers. For fifteen years, we have run a small Sufi Center from the spare bedroom of our apartment in Yonkers, New York. Just a few students, some of whom you will meet later on in this book, come to our center once a week to meet and share and meditate. There are about 115 Sufi Order International Centers in the United States today, many of them very small like ours; there are somewhat more than two thousand Sufi Order International members in the United States as a whole, with perhaps an equivalent number in Europe and a few hundred in India and other countries (there are also about a dozen other, non-Sufi Order International orders in the United States).

Majida and I and the other field workers do our work quietly, with little fanfare. Those who come for instruction and communion do so because they are compelled by an inner voice to be with others who share their need for personal growth and fulfillment. What does that mean? I will now tell you.

I wander thro' each charter'd street,
Near where the charter'd Thames does flow,
And mark in every face I meet
Marks of weakness, marks of woe.
—William Blake

The Angel that presided o'er my birth
Said, "Little creature, form'd of Joy and Mirth,
"Go love without the help of any Thing on Earth."
—William Blake

Happiness alone is natural and is attained by living naturally.
—Hazrat Inayat Khan

1

HAPPINESS

The other night I was watching the movie *Ghostbusters II* for perhaps the tenth time—you know, the one where ghosts and evil spirits wreak havoc on Manhattan. And as usual I had a good laugh at the mayor's line, "Being miserable and treating people like dirt is every New Yorker's God-given right!"

Since I had lived in New York City for thirty years, I could fully appreciate the comment. New Yorkers even tend to take pride in this image. But being miserable and unhappy would be lots of fun if only it did not hurt so much. Living in the city, I saw, felt, experienced, and sometimes participated in deep unhappiness. I often experienced the pain a perfect stranger was feeling—not its source, but its intensity. This was always hard on me; it got me right in the gut, almost as if it were happening to me—which, in a way, it was, when you consider that all of us are a single entity in the state the Sufis call *Wahdat Al Wujud*, or the Unity of Existence.

Unhappiness is universal. We all experience it, and we all work at alleviating it. Or we get so used to it that it becomes our natural state, and we get confused by moments of happiness and tend to reject them. Or we become accustomed to what we use to alleviate unhappiness—drugs and alcohol, for instance—and get stuck with waging that particular battle in ourselves. Apparently, this is all part of the human condition; unhappiness is the rule—or so we think. The best thing we can say about unhappiness is that when we experience it, we come to understand what happiness is.

THE NATURAL STATE OF THE SOUL

But what do we mean by happiness? As I explain later on, when we use a word in the mystical sense—which is what I am doing here—we often mean something different from the ordinary sense. With this in mind, let's begin our definition of happiness by saying what happiness is not. It is not pleasure, sexual, gastronomic, or intellectual. It is not euphoria or ecstasy, although these may be involved. It is not satisfaction—at a job well done, for instance—though again this may also play a role.

The best definition I know of happiness, and one Hazrat Inayat Khan used frequently, is that it is the natural state of the soul.

By the natural state of the soul, I mean that state of being in which we see all events and conditions as a part of the being of God.

Hazrat Inayat Khan writes:

Earthly pleasures are the shadows of happiness because of their transitory character. True happiness is in love, which is the stream that springs from one's soul; and he who will allow this stream to run continually in all conditions of life, in all situations however difficult, will have happiness which truly belongs to him, the source of which is not without, but within. If there is a constant outpouring of love one becomes a divine fountain, for from the depth of the fountain rises the stream and, on its return, it pours upon the fountain, bathing it continually. It is a divine bath, the true bath in the Ganges, the sacred river. When once one has got the key of this fountain, one is always purified, every moment of one's life; nothing can stay in the mind causing man unhappiness! For happiness alone is natural, and it is attained by knowing and by living naturally.

If this is true—if happiness is the natural state of the soul—why is it so difficult to achieve? One reason is that we are usually in a poor state of communication with our soul. Usually we do not even know that our soul exists. We tend to confuse our personality with the soul. But it is something quite separate and different. We need to work hard at opening a channel to the soul. This is the path of meditation, of Sufism.

I have no idea why God made it so hard for us to be in touch with our soul. Certainly, being immured in the physical body does not help. Our physicalness has persuaded our personality that we need to be bombarded by external stimuli in order to enjoy the worldly pleasures of which Hazrat Inayat Khan speaks above. Our soul, however, knows that true happiness comes from within.

Let's suppose that we have been able to open a channel to our soul. Let's even suppose that we live in constant communion with our soul; that is quite possible. The problem, then, is that to the extent we live in constant communion with our soul, we are never quite able to get very much done of value on the earth plane.

Cleaning house, for example, is out (guys like that one): "Sorry, honey, can't do the dishes right now. I'm communing." Driving a car is definitely out. Talking to people is completely out—actually, not completely out, but the other person has to be in the same place you are or communication will be difficult.

In the state of deep meditation in which we are one with the soul, our personality has to step aside; it must not interfere. This is another one of those mysteries God has laid on us, but that's the way it is. A state of communion with the soul feels wonderful, and is achievable, but it does not help us with the rent or the mortgage payments. I am not saying that going into deep meditation has no usefulness in the world. It is, after all, what a meditator is ultimately aiming for, and its value is incalculable. But as the depth of the reality that lies within us is revealed, how we react to the external world changes, and a shift takes place in the way our personality sees itself. There is always this problem, then, that on the one hand we have a soul whose natural state we aspire to experience and even become, and on the other hand we have a personality that constantly seeks to turn us away from this communion toward the outer world.

How do we reconcile the two? In the above quotation, Hazrat Inayat Khan is saying that the key is to allow the love stream to flow. We must bring our feelings of resentment, of guilt, of inadequacy under control. Perhaps you can think of these feelings as valves or choke points you control, even though you are vague about operating procedures. A good deal of spiritual discipline consists in locating these valves in ourselves and turning them to the proper positions—then remembering the locations so we can go back and do it again, as often as is necessary, until the valves dissolve and the love stream flows unimpeded.

You cannot achieve conscious control of these valves and choke points until you find out who you really are, as opposed to who you think you are. Who you think you are—your image of yourself—is constructed from what you do during the day and the extent to which your actions serve your ego; it is molded by the directions in which your self-pity drives you; it is defined by whether you are victim or victimizer, whether you are domineering or submissive, and by how much you expect from those around you.

The self-image that has been formed in us by our parents, by society, by religion, and so on, may not conform at all to who we really are. If, for example, we think we are really quite loving, while the truth is that we are actually rather nasty, then we will not be able to neutralize our nastiness valve because we will not know that that nastiness valve is there to be neutralized. We must first of all take control of our self-image, by recognizing what is true and what is false about that self-image; only then can we adjust our valves and choke points so that the love stream can flow. We are so much bigger than the forces that made us who we think we are; in learning to access that bigness, we find out who we really are and gain the capability of properly adjusting the valves. To be in balance is one attribute of happiness. How do you achieve that balance? By doing your meditations and your practices. By watching your breath.

You will be amazed by how many questions I answer by saying: "Do your practices, watch your breath." It is not enough just to be a good person; if it were, everyone who was kind to dogs or children would be a mystic. The states described by Hazrat Inayat Khan and Pir Vilayat are interrelated; you could almost say that working on one of them is like working on them all (this is not quite true, but it is true enough). If you are doing the work, the happiness that is your birthright will come.

Hazrat Inayat Khan writes:

One does not take initiation for the sake of attaining happiness. It is true that one cannot attain wisdom without deriving a certain advantage from it, as it is more advantageous to be wise than ignorant. But it is not for this that the journey is entered upon. However, as he progresses on the spiritual path the Sufi becomes aware of a wonderful peace, which inevitably comes from the constant presence of God.

Many people of various beliefs and faiths have written about the practice of the presence of God, and all speak of the happiness they receive from being in His presence. So it is no wonder that the Sufi also, should he wish to speak of it, should testify to similar happiness. He does not claim to a greater happiness than his fellowmen, because he is a human being and subject to all the shortcomings of mankind. But at the same time others can decide about his happiness better even than his words can tell it. The happiness which is experienced in God has no equal in anything in the world, however precious that may be, and everyone who experiences it will realize the same.

You will notice that Hazrat Inayat Khan says we embark on the meditative journey to become wise and that happiness is merely a byproduct of that journey. Hazrat Inayat Khan speaks of the sense of the presence of God that inevitably comes upon us when we advance along the path. When he speaks of this "constant presence of God," he means, I think, that we increasingly come to recognize that all things are a part of the being of God. This sounds nifty, and it is nice to think about—but it is also rather daunting, don't you think?

So you will not be intimidated by the prospect of coming more and more intimately in contact with ultimate reality as you pursue the path of meditation, I suggest you start with smaller thoughts. Hazrat Inayat Khan writes, "Happiness lies in thinking or doing that which one considers beautiful."

Now, that is easier, don't you think? I will give you an example of what I mean. A student came to me once, very down on himself. I will not go into the details, but he thought he was

the pits, the dregs of humanity. I gave him practices and meditations, but every time he came back, he told me he had not
been able to get into them.

After this had gone on for several months, I told him to go
to a museum and look at the beautiful paintings, go to a zoo
and enjoy the animals, seek out a natural setting and enjoy it.
This worked. His condition improved. He had needed to get
used to the idea that beauty exists in the world. If your mind
is focused on beauty and you are suddenly confronted with an
ugly situation or an unpleasant person, you can choose between
ugliness and beauty because your mind has once been serene in
the contemplation of beauty.

THE PRESENCE OF GOD

Now we come to the tricky part—a part I am not sure I am
competent to talk about. Reject what I say if you wish. An
awareness of the presence of God is not a given in our lives.
Physical reality can seem to be quite "other" than the presence
of God; circumstances both internal and external can virtually
block out our experience of that presence, even though all of
reality is a part of the essence of God. Being in the presence of
God really means being a lens through which God looks at the
physical universe. You have always possessed the quality of being a lens, but you may not have been aware of the presence of
God before because the optical quality of your lens was not so
good. Once you have become aware of God's presence in your
life—once you have acknowledged that presence—then that
state of mind polishes the cloudy lens that is you, and you become aware, if only for a moment, that God is looking through
your eyes. It is at this moment that the higher and lower aspects
of your being meld into a single essence.

In the first quotation, Hazrat Inayat Khan is saying, I believe, that the more we do the work of the spiritual school we have chosen, the better we become at refining and polishing the lens that is ourselves. As we do the work, an innocence grows within us that replaces the learned or assumed cynicism with which most of us face the world. Innocence is an essential component of our experiencing the natural state of the soul. That experiencing is happiness.

How do we achieve this state? We do our meditations!

And we watch our breath.

You need to avoid performing what Pir Vilayat called a Spiritual Bypass Operation, that is, assuming you are in a state of spiritual advancement you are not—and in fact cannot be, since you have not done the work required to be in that advanced state. If, for example, you do a few spiritual exercises and then run around telling everyone how incredibly happy you feel, you have missed the point. You may even have a brief experience of the soul's sovereignty and begin to assume you have arrived. But you will have to get comfortable with the fact that you are just beginning. Happiness actually depends on a certain level of spiritual maturity, on a calm knowledge of purpose and potential that you can access at will. That, in turn, depends on the control of the breath. Hazrat Inayat Khan says, "As a horse can be controlled and directed by getting the reins in hand, so life can be controlled and directed by gaining control over breath. Every school of mystics has, as its most important and sacred teaching in the way of attainment, the control and understanding of the mystery of breath."

Exercise 1: Balancing the Breath

Here is a practice that is frequently given to newcomers. Though it is a beginning practice, and it may seem very simple, it has the power to change completely your out-look, your attitude, and your being. The practice consists merely of counting while breathing. If you feel your pulse or your heart beat as you do this, so much the better. But it is not absolutely necessary. What is necessary is the ability to maintain a regular beat as you count.

As you inhale, count to four. Then exhale and count to four. Inhale, four; exhale, four. That's it—except that you do it continually, every spare minute, until it becomes so automatic that you no longer think about it. Then you have balanced your breathing. Though breathing practices can be much more elaborate, they all stem from this simple exercise. First you have to master the art of balanced breathing.

If you have already done this, you can now move on to the next stage: practicing balanced breathing while you walk. As you walk, inhale four steps, then exhale four steps. Choose whatever pacing you find comfortable.

This is balance in action.

This is the kind of exercise I have in mind when I talk about watching the breath. Doing exercises like this is an essential component of spiritual attainment. The other essential component is doing those exercises religiously (no pun intended).

When I meet students from different paths, like Buddhism or Christian mysticism, I note that if they have been doing their exercises regularly for a period of years, there is a certain affinity between them and me, one that transcends any differences we may have in theological outlook. It almost does not seem to matter what discipline you follow as long as you actually follow it. You find the path you personally resonate to, and you follow that path. It is a waste of time to swear allegiance to a teacher or discipline and then not follow through. When you do not follow through, all you do is swell the ranks of some organization and give yourself something to talk about at parties. Happiness is not attained by joining; it is attained by doing.

A student once confided to me she could no longer make herself do her prayers and practices as often as she thought she should. She was a Muslim, and regularity in prayers is important to Islam; the prescription is five times a day. She had been doing her Islamic prayers five times a day for twenty years, but now she found them hard to do. Every time she tried, she felt inadequate. This made her very depressed. We decided she was experiencing the normal reluctance of the personality to change its ideas about itself. She had taken initiation in the Sufi Order and had added to her normal regimen of Muslim exercises the spiritual exercises I was now assigning her. These exercises were beginning to affect her. She thought of herself as religious. But these new spiritual exercises were changing her inner being and therefore changing her surface ideas of what it meant to be religious. All this change was making her grumpy. I told her to continue doing the practices and prayers regardless of how they made her feel. This made her happy; it reinforced what she had already been thinking.

My Muslim student's reaction was a normal one to doing spiritual exercises. We think we are being religious or holy or spiritual or whatever, and all of a sudden we are confronted with the reality of what spirituality is actually doing to our inner being—that is, bringing it forth, empowering it. Then we suddenly have to face the possibility of really changing. "Oh, no!" we cry. "Not that!"

A response of this sort means, of course, that we enjoy being unhappy. After all, unhappiness is a state we are completely familiar with; it is one we know all about and therefore are very reluctant to let go of. Our state of unhappiness is fiendishly clever at thinking up reasons why we should not let go of it. We even tend to be proud of this state; after all, we invented it. And for its part our state of unhappiness is perfectly willing to accept the compromise of appearing in the guise of happiness on the surface while down below it continues to look at things in its old morbid fashion.

THE IMPORTANCE OF COMMUNITY

It is in this connection that the importance of a community of like-minded individuals becomes apparent. Imagine that despite your penchant for clinging to unhappiness, you manage to see some value in the spiritual order you have joined, and that in a determined way you decide to participate regularly in whatever the Order has to offer. Chances are that there will be others like you in attendance, others who will have a greater or lesser aptitude for coming to know their inner beings. Hopefully, the teachers themselves will be good at tapping into their happiness, at allowing the love stream to flow.

Seeing all this, you and your unhappiness can react in several ways. You can get annoyed. You can get angry at the teacher or someone you perceive as being close to the teacher; you can vent your anger, or let it seethe inside you. You can decide that you do not like all this happiness flying around but that you will grit your teeth and bear it anyway, because you have taken a vow.

You can decide that you will try to imitate those who seem better able than you are to access their inner being, and you will stand next to them in class as much as possible. You can combine all the above and add a few wrinkles of your own. It does not matter all that much—except to you, of course—what your inner turmoil is all about, because you have truly decided that you will follow through regardless. Doing some or all of this will give you the opportunity to observe and absorb. That is the core of the student-teacher relationship: the student watches and copies and tries to imitate the teacher in all things. That is why so many students of spirituality seem to be clones of the teacher: they take this imitating to extremes. That is not necessarily a bad thing, since changes really do take place within the student, even though it looks to an observer as if the changes are taking place only on the surface and have to do with dress and speech and so on. But imitation breeds authentic change within, because the student is also observing things like how the teacher relates to the outside world and what the source is of that teacher's inner peace.

Another reason for being regularly in the presence of the teacher and more advanced students is simply to be able to absorb, on an unconscious level, the energy around you. If you hang out with such people long enough, you will begin to be affected by what they do and how they feel. Naturally, you can reject the energy you seem to be absorbing and continue to feel miserable. I have seen many people do that. They need to be around people who have a degree of spiritual contentment, but they are so invested in their own unhappiness that they simply refuse to go the next step of allowing the absorption process to proceed. These are the people who flit around the peripheries of spiritual groups pretending to be committed while never actually making the commitment, promising they will take the next step but never actually doing so. I think that often these people have been so damaged by their lives that they simply cannot imagine feeling whole; such a concept is beyond their ken. If that is the case with you, perhaps seeing a good therapist is in order—not because you are incapable of breaking through, but because you need a lot of help in doing so and the presence of a teacher will not be enough.

If you allow the presence of the teacher and the advanced students to permeate your being, you will discover this kind of exposure helps you change. If you hang out with happy people long enough, you will become happy, too. It is like playing chess with good chess players; you may never be as good as they are, but your playing will certainly improve. In a similar way, merely engaging with God has a profound effect. When you ask the divine a question, the very asking changes you. What I mean is that if you ask God what to do—how you can experience happiness, for instance, or what conditions have to come forth for you to experience happiness—or if you simply ask God to create the conditions within your being that will allow the love stream to flow, you will be different. Your "playing" in the course of life will improve.

There are many reasons why prayer is so extraordinarily powerful, but the main one is that in the act of prayer you allow yourself to become a supplicant. It might be said that those who truly desire the love stream to flow within them and are willing to submit to the personality modifications that are required have put themselves in a powerful position. They have acknowledged the possibility that happiness exists, that they can experience it, and that, even though they may not know how to do so on their own, they are willing to learn. Can you see the power in this attitude?

Stop reading for a moment and think about your access to the inner stream of love. Allow yourself to know what is real, to go beyond your feelings of guilt and inadequacy and just to know what is real. Now, think of how you might formulate a question to God—a supplication, a plea, a simple statement of what you are looking for. Then ask the question and see what happens. The answer may take a while in coming, but God always answers. Just be patient—and remember to follow through on that vow you made to God.

The initiate takes a vow in his heart to make use to the best of his ability of all he receives from the Sufi teaching and practices, not using any parts for selfish purposes.

—Hazrat Inayat Khan

2

COMMITMENT

Once I had been initiated, I found myself in that never-never land where you know you have done something significant with your life but you are not sure what.

I still thought of myself as a hippie, living on the edge, never taking society too seriously. When I mention this to my younger students now, they giggle, but we took being a hippie very seriously back in the '70s. What was my life like then? I had a room in a boarding house with a shared kitchen where I fixed my own meals. I worked as a carpenter for a small construction firm. I drove a rusty black 1965 Nova that used prodigious amounts of oil and left a contrail like a jet plane. I went out with a girlfriend from England who was very sweet and whose name and additional details I will not reveal out of respect for her. This was the girlfriend who took me to my first Pir Vilayat seminar, for which I am eternally grateful, and if I knew where she was now, I would tell her so.

Since I was living in Boston, I started taking classes at the Sufi Center there, and I was soon deep into basic Sufism. But something was missing. It was July 1979, and at the time the Sufi Order had a community house called the Khanaqa as-Safiya on East Fourteenth Street in New York City (*khanaqa*, or *khanqah*, is a Farsi word meaning a house or abode of Sufis and dervishes). I was asked to live at the Khanaqa as-Safiya and help prepare a three-day symposium that Pir Vilayat would be hosting.

It was while I was living in the khanaqa that I met the love of my life. Back in my other, pre-Sufi, existence, I had once had a vision—a vision of a woman. It was a strange sort of vision, because the woman hardly seemed real at all. It was as if I experienced the soul of this woman, her very essence. I felt it had to be my imagination, that there could not possibly be anyone like her for me. And besides, I was married. I dismissed the vision as a self-generated fantasy; I rationalized it as the yearning for the idealized Beloved that we all have. But I did not forget it.

As it turned out, the woman of my vision was living at Khanaqa as-Safiya. I did not recognize her at first for the simple reason that she terrified me.

I should explain that New Age spiritual organizations tend to attract a certain type of man. I do not mean the macho type we associate with beer, belching, and basketball. I mean the more sensitive type—gentle, understanding, and decidedly noncompetitive. Strange to say, the women I have known in New Age groups tend to look upon this type of man with what seems to be amused disdain. I have always found this puzzling, since the cultural message to men for some time now has been to be more sensitive. I find it all the stranger in that attendance at New Age groups is about 75 percent women; you would have thought, given the odds, that any man in such a group might find a partner. But women in New Age groups seem to prefer macho men. Perhaps some kind of genetic imperative is at work here; perhaps the women's spiritual genes need to be balanced by macho genes for the sake of offspring.

At any rate, I became aware of this phenomenon the moment I entered the Order. I was used to guys who could do things; it is hard to be a hippie/back-to-the-land type if you cannot fix your car or chop wood or think politically. I was not used to men who cannot do anything, who in fact should not be allowed to own tools, and who think time well spent is when you are talking about your feelings. Not that there is necessarily anything wrong with talking about your feelings. But all the time?

I was also used to macho-type women who can fix cars and chop wood and think politically. What I had not expected was the superabundance of spiritually inclined women who were after wood-chopping men. This terrified me. Maybe some other guy would have viewed the situation as a big opportunity and taken advantage of it, but not me. I had just gotten over a wife, then a girlfriend, who had left me, and I found all too daunting the experience of being a prime side of beef at the center of a circle of hungry female wolves. I did my best to ignore the slavering jaws and burning eyes and tried to settle down to learning about Sufism. But Majida, the woman of my vision, was there. She herself had had a vision of a man in the same way as I had had a vision of a woman—and that man was me. I like to think now—the thought would have terrified me at the time—that she stalked me like one of those female wolves I just mentioned. But her reaction was more like, "Oh my God, what do I do about this?" So we circled each other, I oblivious, she chagrined, until finally we got together. This mutual circling afforded a good laugh to some of the more sophisticated members of the khanaqa.

I was not terrified only of these women. I was also terrified of New York City. I am a country boy, raised in Minnesota, and I had lived in rural settings most of my life. Now I was in New York City, and I had no city moves. I also had vocabulary problems, self-awareness problems, and money problems, and I tended to be morose and wallow in self-pity—or so I was told more than once. Many times, in fact. So I had all this to contend with, and I was truly rattled. But I also had a job that I had agreed to do, and I was determined to do it.

That job was to be a Sufi. I had taken a vow.

I had all the hang-ups I have listed above, plus a few more I will not mention, but through it all I was aware that I had taken a vow—two vows, in fact. One was to the Sufi hierarchy. The other was to Pir Vilayat. There was no way I was not going to follow through on this twofold vow.

The Need for Commitment

We find it easy to make a commitment these days. We know that we do not really have to mean it, that we can decide at any time not to follow through, or we can decide it was all a mistake.

Maybe we are lax about commitment because we are so used to being fooled. We have been lied to so often by the society we live in—by our government, by our religious leaders, by our teachers, by the media, sometimes by our families—that we do not know who to believe anymore. If you cannot believe anybody, you can easily reverse any decision you make simply by saying, "They lied to me." That is an acceptable excuse these days. We hear it all around us, and we see it backed up in the uninterrupted parade of Hollywood conspiracy-theory movies that appear on TV and pass through our movie theaters. For years after I joined the Sufi Order, I struggled with the belief that spirituality was some sort of scam. The struggle got particularly intense whenever I was on the verge of making a breakthrough.

There was always a part of me that wondered if the whole thing were not just a hustle. But sometimes the commitment we make is the right one. This is difficult to see today, because we have to throw off so many years of social conditioning; it is all the more difficult to see when we are trying to make a commitment to something society regards as marginal. Such was my situation: I was living in the khanaqa on East Fourteenth Street in New York City, in the same house with my new girlfriend, whom I considered to be so very special, and I was doing battle with all that societal conditioning that considered Sufism, along with so much else that is valuable, to be marginal and possibly a scam. But, in a way, I was not struggling at all, because it had not been the strange, far-out ideas of the Order that had attracted me to Sufism. It had been the light of my teacher. What Pir Vilayat was saying, the vibrations he gave forth, seemed to me to have the authentic feel of truth. But ultimately what drew me into his presence day after day was the way he said things that I found I could believe—that, and a voice inside me that kept saying, "This is your teacher."

To put it another way: before I met Pir Vilayat, I had already begun to ponder in my limited way the ideas he seemed to embody, and I needed him to complete what I had begun in my own halting way within myself.

The ownership by the discredited guru Bhagwan Shree Rajneesh of ninety-three Rolls-Royces has come to be the scarlet letter of what conventional society thinks of gurus. But whenever Pir Vilayat visited us, there was not a Rolls-Royce to be seen. Naturally I had come to the center with an enormous number of society-ingrained prejudices about the way gurus really are. But first, there was nothing at all like that about Pir Vilayat. And second, it did not matter. All those things—the

prejudices of society, my ideas about what a center would be—
all of them faded away once I had decided Pir Vilayat was my
man. Then, I readily took my vow.

THE LIFETIME VOW

The vow is for life. It has to be; how can you find out if what you
have dedicated yourself to works if you regard it as a stopgap
measure, something you are doing till something better comes
along? Let me illustrate with a Sufi story:

A traveling sheikh was famed for the grace and power of his
blessing. One day, he arrived at a certain village, and, as was
customary, all the villagers came out to greet him and to receive
his blessing.

This day, however, this sheikh, who was preternaturally per-
ceptive, sensed that one of the villagers was missing. He asked
the other villagers who this person was and why he had not
come to be blessed. The villagers replied that the missing man
was Achmed, and that he never went to see a teacher without
his own teacher's permission. They added that Achmed's teacher
had died, and that ever since then he had absolutely refused to
see any other teacher. This caught the sheikh's interest. He went
to see Achmed and asked him if this were true. Achmed replied that it was and explained that his feeling of loyalty toward
his teacher was such that, even though the teacher was dead,
he could not conceive of receiving the blessing of any other
sheikh. The visiting sheikh thought this was admirable, and he
told Achmed so. He also told him that he had known Achmed's
teacher and that this man had not been a true man of God but
in reality a charlatan, and that when he had died he had gone
not to heaven but to hell.

Achmed was not the least bit fazed. He told the sheikh that he had always known his teacher was a charlatan but that that had nothing to do with his loyalty toward him. He would continue to revere the memory of his teacher even though this might mean that he would eventually have to join him in hell.

The sheikh was very pleased at Achmed's reply and went away to bless the rest of the villagers.

Now, that is a serious commitment!

There is a limit, though. You have to be wary of the real wacko, like the ones who release poison gas in the subways of Tokyo or the ones who insist that only white people have rights because—well, who knows why, but I am sure they think their reasons are good ones.

When you make a real commitment, it is something that only you know about. You cannot tell somebody about it who does not have it; it will make no sense to that person. Somebody who does have it will simply say, "Well, of course." Real commitment is something that either you have or you do not have. It seems to be a function of who you are, and it is something that cannot be forced.

If you are worried because you cannot commit yourself to anything, maybe it is because nothing has come along so far that really inspires you. On the other hand, if you are good at commitment, if you are already committed to your family or your profession or to an avocation that you genuinely love, then the step into making a spiritual commitment will potentially be an easy one for you.

All you have to do is decide how far you want to push the envelope of your beliefs.

I mean by this that when you commit yourself spiritually, your personality will not completely understand what you do.

In committing yourself, you may be quite happily prepared to drop the concept of God that was inculcated in you as a child in favor of what you are sure is the deeper divinity of the God of the spiritual group.

But, even if you have no trouble dropping the God of your childhood, your personality will demand that you begin the journey on the path with at least some concept of God. Your personality will demand that you invent a new image of God, and, almost inevitably (because this is the only way your personality can feel comfortable), your new God will have some of the trappings of the God you left behind.

TOWARD A NEW GOD

Perhaps you will invent a God of retribution; perhaps you will invent a God of compassion; perhaps you will invent a God of love. All this is fine. The trouble is that none of your inventions will resemble the God of Sufism.

According to Ibn 'Arabi, the names of God are infinite, but God has ninety-nine specific names that are attributes that are actually mentioned in the Koran. A number of these name/attributes actually appear rather negative to our Western Christian eyes. For example, one of God's names in Islam is *Al Darr*, or "He Who Distresses," and another is *Al Khafid*, "He Who Abases."

You and I would probably prefer a God who is exclusively compassionate, one who would not hurt a kitten, let alone cause a human being distress. We in our culture have a difficult time with a God who watches over a universe of interactions of physical, emotional, and spiritual energy with an air of amused tolerance.

In the light of the unknown nature of God, you may want to make things easier for yourself by focusing your commitment a bit, by stating just what it is you want from this commitment.

Is it personal transformation that you want? Is it peace for the world?

My own favorite want is dying consciously; I am training myself to be able to make a conscious transition from this world to the next when I die. I do not like the idea of going fearfully into the night, of slipping into the next level of existence in a state of paralysis (whatever the nature of that next level may be). So part of the reason I work so hard on meditation and spirituality is so that, when the moment of death comes, I can be awake enough to enjoy the whole thing. Being concentrated on this goal of dying consciously, which I want so badly to attain, helps me overcome the momentary tremors I feel as I advance along the spiritual path that is ever unknown, though it is ever unfolding to knowledge.

Hazrat Inayat Khan writes:

> It is the ideal which prompts man to sacrifice, and the most important thing he can sacrifice is his own life. A man without ideal has no depth; he is shallow. However pleased he may be with his everyday life, he can never enjoy that happiness which is independent of outer circumstances. The pleasure which is experienced through pain is the pleasure experienced by the idealist. But what of the pleasure that has not come out of pain? It is tasteless. Life's gain, which people think so much of, what is it after all? A loss caused by an ideal is a greater gain than any other gain in this world. You must find your ideal in yourself; no ideal in life will prove lasting and true except the one you yourself make.

Another way of pushing the envelope consists in looking at yourself and gauging the extent of the depths within you. Many people seem shallow, and many people *are* shallow—but that is only because they have not yet accessed the depths in themselves. In making a commitment to meditation and spirituality, you have to decide how deep you are going to dare to be, how mighty the goals are going to be that you set yourself, in this universe where everything is possible. As Hazrat Inayat Khan states above, you must create the most profound ideal you can, one whose pleasure will likely be born out of pain.

Exercise 2: Imagining the Master

Get into as quiet a space as possible.

Balance your breath; breathe in and out evenly and regularly. Note that, as you do so, your breath automatically slows down. It will take a little work to learn how to do this; do not be discouraged if slowing the breath seems elusive.

When you feel relaxed enough, turn your attention to a master or a saint or a great being whom you admire. See if you can identify what it is about that being that you find so appealing. Is it the person's historical activity? Is it something you imagine to be true about that person's essence?

Is it a feeling you have that that being feels a closeness to you, as if there were some connection between the two of you? Whatever it is—and it could be a combination of things—see if you can find these attributes in yourself.

There is a slight variant on this exercise that consists of your trying to imagine that you are authentic, whole, and capable. You do this by choosing a sheikh or guru or some other spiritually accomplished person with whom you are familiar and then imagining what it is like to be that person. Remember that such persons are human, after all, and that they have their own quirks. Imagine that they exude a certain awareness that is both charming and compelling. I am speaking here of a living person, not a prophet or a master from the past. Try to imagine how these great persons experience their own energy. Imagine that you possess a similar energy, or aspect of spirituality, but in a way that is more appropriate to your particular quirks.

The idea behind this exercise is that you cannot identify a quality in somebody unless you have that quality in yourself. Ordinarily, this idea is used to show that we have the same capacity for foibles and sin as someone else, but it can also be used to demonstrate that we are great beings. What you are doing here is creating an ideal Self within yourself, and dedicating yourself to the unfolding of this ideal Self. You will have to push the envelope of your concept of yourself very hard to include this new discovery, and you will have to push it even harder to accommodate the new sense of being that will make it a reality.

Note that the part of you that is reading this book and judging whether or not you measure up to the above is your personality, your surface sense of yourself. True commitment comes from deep within ourselves. The surface sense of self has the option to give way to this depth; it can table its criticisms and judgments and adjust its attitudes and perceptions so as finally to allow the deeper Self to hold sway.

But this process can take place only if the personality is willing! If you note a massive amount of unwillingness in yourself, it may mean that the time has not yet come for you to make a commitment. It may also mean finally that, as good as it looked at the time, this is not really the kind of commitment that is appropriate for you; it may be that not only your personality, but your inner Self as well, is resisting. If this is happening, your inner Self may have cause.

Examine your situation carefully. Other reasons for resistance may be terror, or fear of the unknown, or fear of change—or all the above. This is where the reassurances of a spiritual peer group and a spiritual guide are particularly valuable; their presence means you are not conducting your spiritual journey in a vacuum. No one in the group will force you or cajole you into doing something you do not want to do; that simply is not done.

THE NONBEING OF SEPARATENESS

The older I get, the more aware I become of how isolated we human beings feel ourselves to be, no matter what our circumstances. Those drawn to the spiritual life, especially, feel this; likely it is because they have been treated as a little odd most of their lives. It is only fairly recently that I have had the experience of directly realizing how precious is our coming together in Sufism. It was when I was at a representatives' camp that I suddenly saw all the people there, whom I had known for years, as the most beloved of my friends and how amazingly important they were to me. Up to that point, I had been so involved in my own psychospiritual meanderings that I had not really noticed anyone else. I now realize that there was an initiation of sorts in my feeling what I felt: that those around me were my most precious family, that they were as much a part of my own growth and even of myself as they were a part of their own growth and of themselves—that we were all aspects of the One Being. Unfortunately, we humans have the habit of feeling isolated; probably we are taught to feel this way. But it is a mistaken feeling.

Commitment can be seen as allowing beauty to enter our lives; as allowing the desire for intimate spiritual expression to come forward and become itself, as the acknowledgment of our capacity for evoking the divine being within ourselves.

I recommend now that you put this book down, slow your breath down in the way I have indicated above, and turn your attention to who you would like to become if you could become who you are. See if you can find the kernel of purity within yourself that is the truth of your essence; then, water it and fertilize it.

This is true commitment: nurturing within yourself the kernel of truth and purity that is what you already are.

Through every condition, agreeable or disagreeable, the soul makes its way towards the goal.

—Hazrat Inayat Khan

3

PERSONAL
PROBLEMS

There is a story about Saint Teresa of Avila, the visionary Spanish nun who lived from 1515 to 1582. She was on the road, traveling by coach to answer questions before the Inquisition. It was night, it was raining, it was muddy, and the coach ran off the road into a ditch. As she extricated herself from the vehicle, Saint Teresa heard a voice proclaiming from the sky: "Dost thou not know, Teresa, that this is how I treat my friends?"

The exhausted saint, her vision blurred by raindrops, looked up into the night sky and shrieked, "It is small wonder, then, that Thou hast so few of them!"

There is no reason to suppose your life is going to get easier just because you have begun to meditate. You may expect this to happen, because one of the come-ons of meditation classes is stress reduction. This works, I suppose; but stress-reduction meditation is not meditation but breathing and relaxation exercises that you have to know to move on to meditation. But it is really just a bare beginning. Pir Vilayat used to chuckle at the whole idea, declaring that this was a very superficial approach.

41

He was very clear in saying that you have to have a better reason to meditate, because once you begin to meditate in earnest, your problems multiply. Personal problems come in all shapes and sizes and levels of intensity, from as simple as a splinter in your finger to as complex as being a refugee escaping from a war. Nevertheless, most personal problems fall into the "I'm not happy" category. Look at your current personal problems and see if they do not all really fall under that heading, even if only partially. Let's choose an extreme example: You were a victim of child abuse, and you have been traumatized because of it ever since. As serious as this may be, it still belongs in the "I'm not happy" category.

I do not mean to be flip. An "I'm not happy" problem is a serious problem. Note how advertising relies on our "I'm not happy" lament to sell things. Just about any advertisement you would care to name promises something better, the attainment of some elusive happiness. Madison Avenue has made billions by recognizing that we all have "I'm not happy" problems and exploiting them mercilessly. So we need to recognize those problems within ourselves, and we need to recognize that they come from *within* us. We tend to see our personal problems as external in origin rather than as self-generated. (And, certainly, some of our problems are external in origin: becoming a war refugee, for example, is hardly a self-generated state and belongs in the accident category: it is a case of being in the wrong place at the wrong time. Besides, war is a category unto itself and one I do not want to deal with extensively in this book.) In many cases our personal problems are such that we should almost consider them a luxury item, especially in the light of the many problems that bedevil the world today. To have a good reason for saying, "I'm not happy," is a whole lot better than having a good reason to say, for example, "I'm starving, and soldiers conscripted my twelve-year-old boy into the army last week."

If you do have the luxury of personal problems, it would be a sin for you to waste this opportunity God has given you. It would be a mistake to think that because people are in distress in Somalia, your personal problems do not have significance. God goes to a great deal of trouble to ensure that there are people in the world who have the luxury of personal problems—and besides, you are not in Somalia.

Moreover, it is a mistake to think that in our world of *maya* (the Sanskrit word for "illusion") we should train ourselves not to be affected by a problem unless it is so huge that we are forced to pay attention. That is silly. It may be maya, it may be illusion—but if you break your arm, I guarantee you that illusion is going to hurt. It is the same with emotional distress: illusion or not, it hurts.

Challenging Our Self-Image

Most people make concessions about the meaning of their lives based on pressures they experience or messages they receive from those around them. A young man, for instance, may secretly desire to be an artist, yet he bows to the family pressure to become a lawyer, burying his artistic ambitions. The concession may be totally out of sync with what is true to his nature, but eventually it becomes comfortable for him. He may even forget that he ever wanted to be an artist.

Once we start meditating, however, our innermost desires tend to resurface, and we begin to feel uncomfortable. At one point, I had a self-pity problem I did not own up to. I created other problems for myself because of my blindness to this problem. Finally acknowledging the problem, however, did not mean it went away. It stayed around—but it got refiled in the embarrassment drawer, so that now when it comes up I have the presence of mind to become embarrassed rather than to indulge in a self-pity wallow. It is helpful to see your problem from as many different angles as possible. If you can detach from your point of view, even if just a little, even if just for a moment, and look at that problem as if it belonged to a friend and was not yours at all, then you might be able to discover aspects of the problem that you had not noticed when you were so intimately wrapped up in it. If the problem involves someone else (doesn't it always?), perhaps it will help to see yourself and the other person as players interacting on a stage. Better still, try getting into the consciousness of the other person, seeing things from his or her point of view (to which, however wholly mistaken you know it to be, he or she persists in clinging for some strange reason). If you can do this, if only for a moment, your whole take on the relationship might change.

Once you have shifted perspective, even if only slightly, you are ready for step two: finding the cause within the cause. In the case of my self-pity problem, the causes within the causes were, in descending order: a feeling of ineffectiveness; a feeling of in-adequacy; a need for attention; confusion about my purpose in life—and, beneath all this, the knowledge that my purpose in life was one of service. Eventually, I was able to trace the source of my self-pity to this unrealized and long-buried need to serve. In this way, personal problems can actually reconnect us to our innermost potential.

I am not saying any of this is easy; you have to work at it. But the key is to admit that maybe your way of seeing things is a touch skewed from the vision of things you came into this world with, that it is a bit distorted from your original desire.

What was that original desire? Why, it was the vow you took before you were born to fulfill your part of God's great plan. It was the thrust of evolution propelling you forward. It was whatever you think it was, as long as that thought is at the outermost edge of what you can conceive.

THE PROBLEM WAS ALWAYS YOURS

A note of caution: While it is true that your original desire survives the transition into incarnation on this planet, still, as our body grows and our personality develops, pollution, or more accurately intoxication, enters the picture. The genetic inheritance from our parents, the environment we are reared in—both serve to modify and distort the purity of our prelife eternity desires. That is how it is. Beats me why God set things up this way, but that is what God did. It does absolutely no good to get into a parent-blaming mode. The problem is yours now. You own it. And while bashing your parents or other relatives (and, as a last resort, God) may give you a certain temporary satisfaction, it is pointless. Going to them and saying, "You really screwed this up in me; now fix it," will not work. If you are going to travel the path of the mystic, understand that certain things must be left behind. You may find that when you are with your family, you have to pretend that nothing within you has changed. You do this simply because to do otherwise would be too upsetting for them. Most of my acquaintances on the path tell me their parents know they are into something odd but never ask about it. Once my mother came to visit me for a few days, saying she would leave on Sunday night. When she discovered I was performing the worship service that Sunday and more or less expected her to attend, she found an excuse for leaving Sunday morning. At the time, this really upset me, but I came to understand that within her world she could do nothing else. To admit I was doing what was so strange to her would have rattled her reality entirely too much. And so she left on Sunday morning.

Hazrat Inayat Khan writes, "The Message is a call to those whose hour has come to awaken, and it is a lullaby to those who are still meant to sleep."

Pir-o-Murshid also says that it is a sin to awaken a sleeper. And so it is. Besides, you usually will not succeed, and you will end up with a hysterical person on your hands. Remember, a lot of what happens on the spiritual path is scary for the personality that has not been prepared to handle it by a hierarchy of teachers. It is even scary for the personality that has been prepared!

Exercise 3: *Shahid*: The Witness

Here is an exercise you can do every day, one that will help you immensely in sorting out the causes of your problems. When you go to bed and enter into the state of reverie known as the alpha state that comes just before sleep, review your entire day. Backward or forward, it does not matter which, but pick one and stick to it; otherwise your subconscious will get confused, and we do not want confusion at this stage. The key is to look at the events of the day without judging your actions or the actions of others. Just look. In Sufism, we call this exercise *Shahid*—The Witness. Shahid is completely neutral in attitude. There is no judgment.

The results of this exercise depend on how good you get at it. As in anything else, you have to work at it, and the harder you work at it, the sharper your perceptions become. The description I have just given is essentially it; no further elaboration is necessary.

MICHAEL

I had a friend named Michael who, if he was not my best friend, was among the top two or three. In 1998, Michael's doctors told him he had type four cancer of the stomach and had only three weeks left to live. It was as if they were thinking, "He's a goner. Now, who's next on our list?" Worse still, Michael agreed. At different times we told him he had a choice: he could give up, or he could fight. Six months later, Michael's prognosis, if not wonderful, was now at least stable. Better still, Michael's attitude was improving and his being was expanding, both visibly. I was happy things were improving for Michael and visited him as often as I could, to cheer him on and because of the great conversations we were having. I could not help feeling, though, that, on an unconscious level, at least, some of our friends were disappointed by Michael's continued survival. They were believers in that strange school of psychology that says that Michael was responsible for his own illness, that he was somehow making himself into a martyr, suffering and dying for the sins of the rest of us. It really got weird. I am ashamed to say that I bought into some of this. I came to my senses when one of the group told me that he had been glad to hear I had shed tears for Michael. What the hell was this person thinking? I wondered. Was it that because I had bought into these "reasons" for Michael's illness, I could not weep for my friend? That is when I realized that Michael was sick—period. That was all there was to it.

No undercurrents of gloom or doom had created his condition. People get sick because sickness is a part of life.

At the same time I realized how myopic our view of life can get. What happened was that our little group of Sufis, of which Michael and I were a part, had gone into a panic. There are only twenty to thirty of us in the group at any one time, and this was the first time any of us had gotten seriously ill. We had had a couple of accidental deaths, but no life-threatening diseases, and now, thrown off balance by Michael's illness, we were desperately searching for an answer. We had to understand—even if it meant assigning two-thirds of the blame to Michael and/or his wife and one-third to ourselves. Somehow, somewhere, fault had to be found.

It seems that the further removed we are from a critical situation, the more likely we are to assign blame. If we are really close to someone who is sick, we just want that person to get well. But the further outside the intimate circle we are, the more likely we are to just get impatient. All of which might lead you to believe that our personal problems loom very large for us, while the problems of others are important only to the extent that our own ego is bound up with them. That is the way it is. This is just another example of how God set things up. If you have a splinter in your finger, all you can think about is getting it out. If the splinter is in someone else's finger, that is that person's problem. You may offer helpful advice, such as, "I have tweezers specifically designed for splinter removal, which I will gladly loan you," but you will probably add, "As for extracting the splinter, that's up to you." This is not far different from how spiritual guides, including myself, regard the personal problems people bring to us, with the one addition (besides the compassion we feel) that we tend to look at those problems with an eye to seeing what new qualities of soul are forcing their way through the morass of personality and in so doing causing the difficulties. The first step in dealing with your problems is to work on seeing how many of them are self-generated. Here is where the practice of reviewing each day comes in handy. You need to review your whole life, watching it as if it were a movie and trying to find places where you made a decision that could have gone any number of ways, but you chose that particular way.

Truth is basic to this practice. You have to learn to look at your life unwaveringly, without excuses. And however tempting it may be, you have to be very careful about turning the light of truth on other people. We seem to feel that, when we discover something about ourselves that is true but unpleasant, we are also under an obligation to point out that unpleasant quality to everyone else who possesses it. Do not do that. Saying "I always tell the truth" is just an excuse for hurting other people. Sufism holds that, given the ultimate reality of the universe, telling the truth is impossible, since we can never know the whole of a thing or even begin to suspect all its ramifications. So, restrict truth-telling to self-examination.

And avoid beating up on yourself. There is this idea, left over from the Middle Ages, that self-flagellation is a necessary adjunct to the pursuit of the mystical life or of any kind of religious or spiritual experience. This is silly. The idea is not self-recrimination but discovering the qualities that are asserting themselves in your being. You will have no trouble knowing what your deficiencies are, because as soon as you start the process of self-examination, they will show up. What a spiritual guide wants for you is that at the same time as you are discovering your many flaws, you should also know your own splendor. We want you to remember that your being is a part of the being of God, and that God desires to get it right, whatever "right" turns out to be. The only way God can get it right is through the process of your Self-realization. Pir Vilayat liked to talk about an inverted-pyramid relationship with God, one in which a sea of energy narrows down to us mortals who are at the (inverted) apex of the pyramid and are the actual focus of the energy, which must of necessity restrict itself to our limited incarnate beings. The more we are able to surmount our self-pity and the opinions of others about ourselves and reality, the more we are able to acquire a conscious, realized knowledge of the degree to which we are involved in this pyramidal relationship with God.

Ibn ʿArabi says that the names of God, of God's attributes, God's qualities, are limitless. You can get some idea of the possibilities by reading the list of Ninety-nine Names of God as they are known to Islam. If your text lists the Ninety-nine Names with lengthy explanations for each one, ignore the explanations and just contemplate the literal English translation. Explanations are always opinions; develop your own explanations.

THE ROLE OF THE TEACHER

Teachers serve the helpful purpose that we can measure ourselves against, not competitively, but comparatively. I will be dealing with the guide/teacher-student relationship extensively throughout this book, so for now I will simply say that this kind of measuring stick can be very useful. And, in the group that surrounds your teacher, you can measure yourself against those of your peers who have gained your respect. Of course, you will be able to measure yourself against your teacher or the individuals you admire in your group only if you are capable of making rational judgments about what you are observing in the actions and exchanges around you.

The best thing for some people is simply to be told, "Here, work on this." At the time, the instruction might not make sense to the student, but if it comes from someone whose intuition the student trusts (hopefully, his or her guide), then that student can simply go along with it and ignore other considerations. For others, it is necessary to be a little more circumspect. The former tends to be my approach as a teacher—though, to tell the truth, I am not sure how much I tend to rely on somebody else's word myself, even my own guide's, if that word is not matched by some sort of intuitive corroboration within me. So, ultimately, the responsibility lies with the student/mureed to decide whether to accept any given instruction.

I really do not concern myself with my own personality all that much, because I have discovered a unit of measurement within that seems to sum it all up. It is this: I used to really be a jerk, and now I am less of one. My jerkdom has decreased as my faith in my inner being has increased. How do I know this? Because Majida says so. Trust me when I tell you never to argue with my wife.

(I should add that I know students who are able to dissect their personalities with accuracy and objectivity. If you are in that group, continue to do so. Do not let anything I say deflect you from doing what you feel is correct for yourself.)

To return to my friend Michael: I do not think his cancer was the external manifestation of an emerging quality or qualities. As I've said, I think he got sick and that sickness is a part of the human condition we all must face to a greater or lesser degree. There is no doubt that the manner in which Michael made his decisions while suffering from the disease reflected emerging qualities. And, in his case, he was able to provide those around him with a series of excellent lessons in how to react positively to severe external circumstances.

Finally, from time to time try to remember that you are a being of light. This is a key concept in Sufism, one that cannot be described but can only be experienced. Our condition of light-being-ness is bigger, much bigger, than any personal problem that can possibly come along and annoy our physical vehicle—bigger, in fact, than the entire physical universe. Whatever made you think you were smaller than your problems?

Think bigger. Much bigger!

He who thinks himself wise, O Heavens, is a great fool.
—Voltaire

4

THE PATH OF
EMBARRASSMENT

Sufism is called the path of the heart and the path of power. It is also called the path of blame and the path of poverty. And it is all these, and more. I like to call it the path of embarrassment. Whatever your spiritual path, initially embarrassment plays a role.

Nobody likes to be embarrassed (except those who get paid for it); generally, we make every effort to avoid embarrassment. We do not mind watching other people being embarrassed; that is why we watch sitcoms (frankly, I never met a sitcom I liked—but that is just me; maybe you think they are great). The fact is that we enjoy being entertained by embarrassing situations, though we would rather avoid being in embarrassing situations ourselves.

However, that is not quite what I am talking about. I am talking about the moment when you look at yourself and are greatly embarrassed to discover that you are a jerk, that you are confused and uncaring and morally ambivalent, that you cannot keep a coherent thought in your head, that you are completely full of yourself, that you are totally steeped in self-pity—pick any or all the above, or make your own list. I am talking about the moment when you suddenly discover that possibly, just possibly, you have something to learn about being a human being.

That moment of discovery is not fun.

Sufism holds that pathways begin to form in our brain from the moment of our birth. These pathways deepen and send out branches and take on different colorations as we grow older. They are our habits of thought, which evolve as our notions about ourselves and our place in the world evolve. Often the habits of thought we have as adults are the result of decisions we make very early in our lives, even when we are toddlers.

Most of us never try to change these pathways. As we grow older, we continue to support those decisions we made as toddlers, never trying to reassess them in the light of maturity. Yet it is our job, once we have become aware of those pathways, to consciously direct or redirect their growth and change their colorations. We have to identify the contents of each pathway to do this, and identifying these contents can result in a great deal of embarrassment. It is very hard to rise above this embarrassment. These lines appear in the writings of the Swedish film director Ingmar Bergman:

"The aerialist said to the actor, 'My job is very dangerous. Every night I risk my life.'

"The actor replied to the aerialist, 'That's nothing. Every night I risk my ego.'"

YOUR OWN TRUTH

In the preceding section, we looked at personal problems and tried to find ways of localizing and isolating the causes of those problems so we could direct or redirect the energies they contained in more positive directions. When you have identified a cause, what you have on your hands is an embarrassment. When you have reflected on this embarrassing quality, you quickly become aware of how interwoven it is with many other parts of your life.

People sometimes come to me in great distress—I am frequently in that condition myself—because they have just discovered some new, disturbing, and very embarrassing truth about themselves. They have found out they are selfish. They have discovered that feelings of contempt play a big part in their emotions. They have realized they are often critical of others for no good reason. They have discovered that they treat their wife, their husband, their children, their dog, their cat, their goldfish, and others, badly.

It makes them very unhappy to see these things in themselves. I tell them:

- The purer we become, the more aware we become of the flaws we have had and have; the holiest of monks knows he is the worst of sinners.
- The fact that these things are coming up at all means that the work you are doing on yourself has been effective.
- Because we have just noticed a flaw does not mean that flaw is new. It may always have been there, but we are just now noticing it, and that means we are just now able to deal with it.

Frustrating, isn't it? You take up meditation expecting to hear celestial choirs singing and see fireworks going off, and what you get is: "I'm a jerk." Maybe at the start you heard an angel singing and saw some fireworks exploding—that often happens initially—but inevitably, if you do the work, what comes up is: "I'm a jerk."

At this point you need to remember how to breathe. Nothing fancy; just pay attention to your breathing. You will notice that just giving attention to your breath slows it down, and that after a while you will feel slightly more in balance. This simple practice of breathing is the foundation of all meditation exercises.

Exercise 4: Paying Attention to the Breath

Here is a practice that will help you pay attention to your breathing. Notice the rhythm as you inhale and exhale. Focus on keeping the rhythm the same. Give some thought to the physical process that is taking place: The oxygen in your lungs is being transferred to the bloodstream, and when you exhale, waste gas is being released. Something like 70 percent of the waste products produced by your body is expelled through the breath.

The next step in this practice can go one of several ways. The two most common are "breathing light," which I describe elsewhere, and thinking of a word or phrase in conjunction with the breath. The latter exercise is called by the Sufis *Darood*. A Darood is a word or a phrase you hold in your mind to replace the usual tape-loops of thought that most of us hold in our minds most of the time. A Darood can be any word or a phrase, from a name of God such as Allah or Brahma, to a simple phrase like "I am calm" or "I am relaxed."

Having done the above exercise, try taking another look at what upset you. Maybe it is not as bad as you thought. Or maybe it is. Either way, something has to be done about it. But what?

JUST SAY NO

I do not want to stray into the territory of psychology. If you have discovered something particularly nasty about yourself, you should probably go to a psychologist. But spiritual guides cannot avoid wandering into the realm of psychology to a certain extent—though, when we do, our approach tends to be more informal.

Let's take something simple. You discover that you are too critical of other people. You might be inclined to defend this trait by saying that being overly critical is a manifestation of a desire for perfection. But your job is not to enforce perfection in other people. It is to enforce perfection in yourself. (You are probably just as critical of yourself as you are of other people.)

So what do you do? You keep it simple. When you feel an attack of being overly critical coming on, do not do it. For a while this may throw a crimp into how you interact with other people. You will have to find a way around that. (I have no idea how you will do it; that is your problem.) Remember, though: keep it simple. You are not performing brain surgery on yourself. All you are doing is noting inappropriate behavior in yourself and stopping it. You find it distressing that you behave this way. Other people find it distressing that you behave this way, because such behavior is inappropriate. So you do not do it.

Do not, repeat, do not, tell anyone you are not doing it. As soon as you tell somebody else you are not doing it, you lose personal power. There is just one person that you can tell with impunity that you are not doing it, and that is your teacher or guide. If they know their business, spiritual instructors will only encourage you in such pursuits.

There is a rule of esoteric wisdom—it is even a rule of conventional psychology—that says that you cannot recognize a fault or a virtue or anything else in another person unless you possess that fault or virtue or whatever else in yourself. When we find fault with somebody else, what we are really doing is merely drumming up a drama to make our own lives more interesting. The less attuned we are to our inner life, the more likely we are to seek out some manifestation of that inner life (or even, however unconsciously, provoke that manifestation) in the external world.

If you have suddenly seen yourself in what I have said, do not go off on a self-pity jag. Remember that the purpose of this chapter is to more-or-less casually list several prominent embarrassments we all have and show how they serve to point out to us what we need to work on in our lives. A little self-criticism is fine. Just do not take it too seriously.

I am sure there is not one of you who, in reading what I have just written—that the faults we bemoan in others are the faults we possess in ourselves—has not just now had acid-type flashes of bits of gossip that he or she has gleefully passed along describing the annoying faults of friends or acquaintances or total strangers, or notorious or not-so-notorious public figures (just think Bill Clinton or George W. Bush). And probably you have just now also been brought face-to-face with the unsettling truth that certain of these attributes emanate straight from you; in short, you have had to admit that all of us, including you, take a certain vicarious pleasure in somebody else's pain, for reasons that I hope I have made clear by now, even if that pain is only the sort that elicits a gentle, "Tsk, tsk."

MISJUDGING YOUR PLACE ON THE PATH

Another prominent source of embarrassment has to do with how far along the spiritual path we think we are. Either we think we are cooler than we really are in terms of our progress, or we seriously underestimate the degree of coolness we have achieved.

It can be hard for us to recognize the first state, since we have usually foolishly proclaimed to one and all the high degree of our coolness and even hinted that we are certainly the peer of everyone in the group and maybe even advanced enough to teach it. It takes a lot of courage to back away from a glowing self-estimate of our worth about which we have informed everybody.

People who really are spiritually aware tolerate this type of behavior, because they know that eventually the exaggerator of spiritual progress will have to face the truth about him- or herself and that some very serious embarrassment will be the result. People who are genuinely spiritually aware understand that this type of misassessment generally stems from a sense of inadequacy; they know that the progress-exaggerators are afraid they do not really know what is going on, or that they are somehow out of the loop. None of us is ever really out of the loop (or, more accurately, the spiral). It is just that we have not been able to access the whole loop yet. If you discover that you have been faking your level of Self-realization, you will just have to swallow your pride and go back to being a student. Often, it is then that you discover something wonderful—that those around you will be totally forgiving of you once you have stopped claiming you possess something you do not yet possess.

As for underestimating the degree of your progress: to tell you the truth, this is something I know about only through

61

observation; personally, I am prone to overestimating my place on the road—which is why I am able to go on at such length about that kind of misassessment.

When I have students who tend to underestimate their progress, I help them by giving them practices intended to enhance their self-esteem. The following is an example:

Exercise 5: Superimposing a Great Being

I ask a student to concentrate on a Great Being and see if there is any way in which the student is able to superimpose that Great Being on his or her own being. Another practice that I often employ is to ask the student to walk like a king or a queen, or an emperor or an empress, perhaps using as examples the archetypes in the Tarot deck (for more information on this practice, see Chapter 13, The Light of Knighthood). I may also ask the student to try to experience the being that is presently being unveiled within him- or herself. You, the reader, can try this if you would like: what you must do is imagine who you are becoming. This is something athletes do all the time: by methodically visualizing their performance before an event actually takes place, they help themselves to perform successfully.

If you are of a spiritual turn of mind, you might tend to believe that this process of visualizing your emerging inner Self is difficult; we are inclined to believe that such inner archetypes are subtle and elusive and remote from the outward self. Nevertheless, that inner being, however subtly it is manifesting within us, is right there inside us, and we should try to experience it. You will not be totally successful, but that's okay. Just imagine yourself as the whole being you desire to be, and see what happens.

There are numerous levels of commitment and understanding, and just because you suspect yours do not measure up to somebody else's does not mean they are not significant in themselves. The other person may simply be more confident or more verbose or more vocally enthusiastic than you—or he or she may not really be farther along the path. If you are the vocally enthusiastic sort, reel it in a bit. You are wasting energy you would be better off saving for something more important than persuading yourself and others that your devotion to the path is exemplary. Remember the old adage:

Those who know, do not talk; those who talk, do not know.

Do not ask about people who write books.

THE HIGHER STANDARD

We teacher/guides in the lower- to midlevel echelons of the Sufi Order sometimes do embarrassing things too; I am sure this is true of other orders. One thing we try hard not to do, however, is get into one-upmanship games where people dance the "I can do anything better than you" dance. Games like this constitute normal human behavior, but the things that happen in a spiritual order have particularly deep and dramatic effects, and this kind of nonsense can be more hurtful in our setting than in an ordinary setting. I have been embarrassed, and I have embarrassed others. All I can do is forgive the former and beg forgiveness for the latter. A group like ours is the last place in the world where you should bear a grudge. One of the pleasures and problems of being a member of the Sufi Order is that we hold ourselves to a higher moral standard than we do the rest of society. The trouble is that we are still a part of that society; it is all too easy for us to forget that we are Sufis and fall back on old patterns of social behavior. In fact, I have sometimes wondered if our higher standards are not simply a set of unreasonable demands, not made entirely in good faith, which give us the unwarranted right to stand in judgment over the behavior of others.

But it is a source of great delight to us when we do things right, when our behavior makes us worthy of being called representatives of the Sufi Order. I cannot describe this delight to you—not will not, but cannot. It is because the members of the Sufi Order strive to adhere to a higher standard than society as a whole that raggedy dervishes can hail each other in all sincerity as King of Kings or Sovereign of the Universe. It took me a long time to understand these things. The closer I get to the upper levels of our Order and the inner circle of its leaders, the more I notice that leaders at these levels do not dance the one-upmanship dance. Each has his or her own separate area of responsibility; they all have enough to do without beating up on each other. (This does not keep the rest of us from trying hard to discover their areas of embarrassment; even Pir Vilayat came in for his share of scrutiny. We can be an irreverent bunch.)

Of course, like any group of this sort, what we do is make manifest internal processes. That does not always redound to our credit, as the following story illustrates:

A man aloft in a hot-air balloon realizes he is lost. He spots a person on the ground, lowers his altitude, and shouts, "Hey! Can you tell me where I am?"

The person below replies, "Yes, you're in a hot-air balloon hovering thirty feet above this field."

The balloonist says: "You must work as a spiritual teacher."

"I do," replies the person on the ground. "How did you know?"

"Well," says the balloonist, "what you've just told me is true enough, but it's of no use to me at all."

The person on the ground says, "You must be a spiritual seeker."

"I am," replies the balloonist. "But how did you know?"

"Well," says the person, "you don't know where you are or where you're going, but you expect me to be able to help you. You're in the same position you were in before we met, but now it's my fault."

Schools that teach esoteric wisdom are basically no different from other schools or organizations. The same human dynamics apply; alpha males and alpha females compete with one another, and everyone else tries to find a comfortable niche.

There is, however, one major difference between a school like ours and an ordinary school. The nature of our work does not allow us to be comfortable. The baseline of our Order is self-criticism or self-interrogation (*Muhasaba*), and it creates a dynamic that constantly surprises.

If, however slightly, you feel a twinge of embarrassment pushing you in the direction of the spiritual path, follow it. You will be led to places you could not have conceived of once and soon will not be able to describe.

All surrender to beauty willingly and to power unwillingly.
—Hazrat Inayat Khan

*If thou desire the presence, union with God Most High,
from him be not absent; when thou visitest thy Beloved,
abandon the world and let it go.*
—Hafez

5

SURRENDER

The word *surrender* has very precise connotations in English, and none of them is very warm or cuddly. The word evokes images of domination by a superior force, or of our being compelled to do something we would rather not do. That is in English. Other languages, I understand, do it differently. A Japanese friend of mine tells me her language has two words for surrender; they are very different in connotation, one meaning what the English word means and the other signifying "the acceptance of love's enfoldment." Other Asian languages probably make the same distinction; but the connotations in English are the only ones I know, and they always send shivers up my spine.

Maybe the idea of surrender is an easy one for you. If so, I applaud your spiritual maturity. As for me, for a long time whenever I heard people in Sufi circles talk about surrender—surrender to the Beloved, for example—my immediate reaction was, "There's no way I'm going to do this thing that I don't even understand!" Admittedly, the phrase "surrender to the Beloved" has a nice poetic ring—but to me it always seemed to imply you were handing power over to whomever this "Beloved" character was.

In fact, that is exactly what it does imply. But there are certain words and phrases that mean one thing in common parlance and resonate with a whole other layer of meaning when they are used in the context of mysticism. "Surrender to the Beloved" is one of those phrases. Surrender to the Beloved certainly has the connotations we customarily assign to it—I mean the ones that send shivers up my spine. But, in the language of Sufism, the meaning is rather different.

WAHDAT AL WUJUD: SUFISM'S DUAL STATE OF BEING

Wahdat Al Wujud is often understood as "the place of no thought," a place Pir Vilayat called "the awakening beyond life." My personal experience of this place is limited, and I am reluctant to describe anything I am not completely familiar with. But here goes, and in what follows I rely heavily on what the Sufi metaphysicians have had to say through the ages. In other words, I do not rely on my own understanding but try to provide you with the distilled wisdom of others. In English, we try to compensate for the harsh undertones of *surrender* by using the phrase *willing surrender*. Willing surrender usually refers to a love relationship (though even here, as my wife points out, we often mean the surrender of a woman's will to the supposedly more powerful, more magnetic, will of the man). But in this chapter I am talking about surrender in the context of spirituality or religion, and in this context we generally mean willing surrender. Even here, though, it seems to imply a surrendering of our puny human will to the all-powerful will of a Creator. For the Sufi, the word *surrender* has a totally different meaning. This is because Sufis believe that human beings experience two completely different but mutually interdependent states of being at one and the same time. This dual state they call *Wahdat Al Wujud*—the "Unity of Existence." Wahdat Al Wujud is a specific condition or, more accurately, a lack of condition, in which all created things are equidistant from the source and have no existence in and of themselves but rather only the potential for self-expression. Selfness—individuation—is irrelevant in this state. To experience Wahdat Al Wujud, you have to go beyond the state of reason, beyond viewing reality as discrete bits of information, and merge with the void of timeless nothingness in which all things have their source and nothing has separate value.

Follow all that? Good! This is the experience of ultimate unity, one that the mystics regularly fail to describe adequately, just as I am now failing to do. Pir Vilayat says this state comes before you realize it and is gone before you know it came. Other Sufis describe it as a place of no thing or The Blackness. All seem to agree that Wahdat Al Wujud is in here, not out there; it is in our being, and we attain it not by searching outside but by diving within. It is a difficult state to describe because we are continually forced to fall back on the vocabulary of the normal everyday world to describe it, and Wahdat Al Wujud is quite beyond our normal everyday world. Sufis get around the difficulty by using metaphor to describe Wahdat Al Wujud. The most common metaphor is that of ocean and waves. In our ordinary conscious state, we perceive Wahdat Al Wujud as waves; we are ignorant that it is an ocean and that that ocean is the source and support of the waves. Though we perceive the waves as discrete objects, they are not separable from the ocean. But in our preoccupation with the shape, the size, the color, the emotional content of the waves, we completely fail to see the ocean. If through meditation and other spiritual practices we can perceive the ocean and merge with it—however briefly, however slightly—the waves begin to recede from our sphere of attention and the ocean begins to become all. This may seem like a desirable state, and it is—except that when we are one with the ocean, we cannot interact with the waves; we cannot get on with the ordinary business of living. Interacting effectively with the waves means giving them most of our attention. This is not hard when we are unaware of the ocean's existence, because then only the waves are real to us. But when we have noticed the ocean, things are never the same for us again.

The Sufis call the state of total immersion in the ocean *Fana* or Annihilation—another word that seems to be negative but really is not. I am quite sure that in my meditations I have never made it as far as Fana, though I understand that there are various levels of Fana, and so it is possible I have brushed against one of the lower rungs of the ladder of ascension to that state; it is hard to tell about these things. But whatever my own experiences, the description I have given more or less conforms to those of the Sufi metaphysicians.

What does all this have to do with surrender?

As you pass through the various levels and planes that lead to the state of Wahdat Al Wujud, or the Unity of Existence, the word *surrender* takes on a whole new meaning. It comes to denote the suspension of our disbelief in a reality other than that of cause and effect. Just for a moment, we stop thinking that we cannot make that ascent, or even that there is an ascent to be made, and we surrender to the infinite space within that knows the state of divine love for what it is. So you see, surrender turns out to be a love relationship—a love relationship willingly embraced. To surrender does not mean to be coerced. You surrender because you cannot conceive of any other outcome for your efforts.

TRADING ADDICTION FOR LOVE

What follows will not seem to be about surrender. But it is. I am going to tell you about how I quit smoking. Or, more accurately, about how I gave up an addiction.

Pir Vilayat always said that giving up an addiction was one of the most powerful acts we can perform, with smoking being one of the toughest to give up. The list of addictions was endless, he said, with his own chief addiction being classical music—not one, he hastened to add, that he was planning to give up!

I believe I was one of the last Sufis in the Western world to give up smoking. Almost everyone smoked when I first joined the Order. The percentage was far greater than for the general population; smoking is a tradition among Turkish Sufis, and a number of us attempted to carry on the tradition. But our numbers dropped off one by one, until there were few smokers left, only me and one or two others. I held out until the very end. I had come to think of myself as the one remaining relic of a bygone era, necessary to the world in the sense that there had to be at least one memento of the age of smoking in some museum somewhere.

Gradually I began to see that my addiction was a silly one, albeit a difficult one to give up. Then, suddenly, all the work I had been doing begin to click in. I had found my own personal guide in the Order; I had been initiated as a retreat guide; I had been meditating in a particular way so as to facilitate my quitting smoking. And my addiction began to ebb. As it did, my libido got reactivated (my wife liked that). At the same time, my inner commitment to Sufism strengthened and steadied.

In giving up my addiction to smoking (it could have been any addiction)—in surrendering that addiction—I had become less dependent on the wave aspect of Wahdat Al Wujud and more open to the inflowing of the ocean aspect. Since that ocean is also an ocean of love, love began to manifest within me in the place of the waning addiction.

The first thing I noticed was that I began to enjoy friendships more. We like to think that we have plenty of friends, and every so often we tally them up (come on, I know you do it; everyone does it, even if only in secret). We want to be able to declare, if to no one but ourselves, that we have, say, four real friends and a slew of acquaintances (the latter of which would become friends in an instant if we only expended the effort). Deep down inside, however, we all secretly wonder if any of these people really are our friends in the way that we think we understand friendship (which leads me to believe that most of us would be happy with just one real friend if we could figure out exactly what friendship was). Our sense of being separate from one another limits the depth of the friendships we can experience. The more we taste of the ocean of Wahdat Al Wujud, the Unity of Existence, the freer we are of the waves of Wahdat Al Wujud—the more we are able to see that another human being is not separate from us at all but is actually a part of us. That is why, as I gradually freed myself from my addiction to smoking, I noted a nifty side effect: friendships were blossoming that I knew were there in potential but that (for fear of rejection, I suppose) I had never pursued. But as I expanded within, I became less worried about rejection and more willing to take chances with relationships. And this has had happy results. It happened because I had willingly given myself over to the natural state of surrender.

Exercise 6: Genuflection and Surrender

How do we cultivate this natural state of surrender? Here is a suggestion: put your head to the floor at least once a day. You can do this by kneeling or lying down. Make this gesture part of your prayers (as do Islam and Buddhism), or make it simply a physical acknowledgment that you are bowing your spirit down before God. Whatever daily regimen you practice, even if it is only a few minutes of reflection, add genuflection to that regimen. You will find this very beneficial. Genuflection puts the body on notice that it is not in control; it puts the mind on notice that it is okay to bow down before a higher power; it puts the spirit on notice that you firmly accept certain principles of spirituality; and it literally as well as symbolically puts the head below the heart and emphasizes the truth that the heart is the greater characteristic of our being.

There are other aspects to pursuing the natural state of surrender. I need to preface what I am about to say by stating that, for the Sufi mystic, the difference between masculine and feminine has nothing to do with gender. The Sufis regard "masculine" as the creative force and "feminine" as the receptive force. They have given these two forces the Arabic names of *Jelal* and *Jemal* respectively. Between Jelal and Jemal, there is the state of *Kemal*.

Kemal may be translated as perfection, but it is a difficult state to understand. Think of it as a point of perfect tension. I often use the example of a basketball player who leaps into the air to shoot the ball. There is a point at which the basketball player is

neither rising nor falling, neither shooting the ball nor not shooting it. This is a point of perfect tension; it is Kemal. When Sufi
metaphysicians describe the creative impulse of the divine, they
call God the Creator Jelal, and the Created Universe Jemal; where
these two meet is Kemal—Perfection. As the Sufis see it, to surrender you must become feminine; you must cultivate the Jemal
aspect of yourself and be responsive to the divine intent.

Moreover, to surrender you must acknowledge that you are
first and foremost a being of light. When you have acquired that
awareness, then, when the Beloved reveals to your light a portion of its light, the natural process of merging gets underway,
and surrender will come about easily.

In the last lines of the Bhagavad Gita, Arjuna says: "By Thy
grace I remember my light, and now it is my delusion. My
doubts are no more, my faith is firm; and now I can say, 'Thy
will be done.'"

You can see that surrender is no trifling act, not anything to
be tossed off like a simple task anyone can perform. (You may
wonder, though, why anyone would want to perform it!) Acknowledging ourselves as beings of light is a means of access to
the world of surrender. Opening this door and keeping it open
is, or should be, one of the great challenges of our lives. But
it is not an easy challenge. Let me give you a spiritual "light"
practice that will help set you on the path to this achievement.
This is the first spiritual practice I ever learned. It is simple, it is
effective, and it is a practice I still follow. I like simple.

Exercise 7: You Are a Being of Light (I)

Imagine the universe is a vast ocean of light that is acces-
sible to you. When you have allowed yourself to imagine

this, breathe, notice the breath as before, and then do the following: On the in-breath, imagine you are drawing a portion of the infinite crystalline light of the cosmos into the top of your head. Imagine you are drawing it through your crown chakra down into your heart (I do not mean your physical heart; I mean your heart center, located behind the sternum). Once you have drawn this light into your heart, you need to do something with it. So, as you exhale, use the intrinsic energy of your heart chakra to transform the crystalline light into a golden light that enhances the light of your aura.

There it is: a nice, simple, effective practice anyone can do. Of what benefit was it? Let's look at what you did. First, you accepted the idea that the universe is basically made of light (you may not be too sure at this point what that means, but you have accepted the idea for now). Then you acknowledged that, just maybe, you could do something with that light (or maybe you cannot, and maybe this is all silliness—but what have you got to lose?).

Then you acknowledged that maybe your body was more than simply a mechanism for digesting fiber and protein and carting your neuroses around in. In fact, you acknowledged that it had at least two centers of energy, the crown chakra and the heart chakra. You further acknowledged that these two centers of energy had the potential of doing something important.

Then you acknowledged that you could direct energy with your breath (maybe you were just pretending you could direct it, but perhaps you were also thinking, Hey, what the heck, maybe it will work). And, finally, you admitted to yourself that there is more to you than just your body and that you have an aura whose brightness you can increase simply by using your will.

You have no idea if any of this is true or if anything really happened to you—but it sounds nice, and maybe it did work, and so maybe you will do it for at least a little while longer.

I have just said a great deal about a supposedly simple practice, don't you think?

Exercise 8: Transforming the Light Energy

You can increase the effectiveness of this practice by adding to it the following (which should be done only when you are sitting still):

Just as before, breathe the crystalline light of the cosmos through your crown chakra down into your heart. At this point, hold your breath and, while rolling your eyeballs up into your head to focus on the third eye, gently place the tip of your tongue on the soft palate. Imagine at the same time that the light you have inhaled into your being has permeated all the molecules of your body, causing them to jiggle and effervesce with the new energy you are supplying them with. Do not hold your breath overlong; there is no need to be uncomfortable. Now, relax your tongue and eyeballs and exhale through your heart, focusing all that transformed light energy through the lens of your heart and flooding your aura with this golden light to enhance and energize it.

It is hard for us to hold in our minds for any length of time the acknowledgment that we are beings of light. This is because we are bombarded every day with the notion that we are a walking, talking, breathing sack of physical matter, plopped down in a universe of similarly constituted sacks, with all these sacks vying for a piece of the earthly action. Doing practices like the ones I have just described will help you overcome this notion.

You will find it helpful to spend time in the presence of those who are better able than you to hold in themselves the knowledge that they are beings of light. It is certainly possible to pursue this goal in a basically isolated manner and, in so doing, successfully improve your spiritual state; look at the many genuinely holy men and women who live the lives of hermits. However, this practice has always seemed to me like a form of self-flagellation. It is not really necessary; and on the whole Sufism limits the act of isolation to a maximum of forty days, occasionally making an exception for those extraordinary individuals for whom there is no other way.

In the ranks of the Sufi Order, there have always been very private persons who hold themselves apart (this is true of other orders as well). It may be that people drawn to spiritual orders are often those who have always been the odd man or woman out. I have always felt very uncomfortable, myself, in group situations that focus on intimate matters. I keep expecting to be told I am doing something wrong; after all, my experience of life has consisted basically of my doing things that did not jibe with the understanding of those around me. This naturally created a hard shell of resistance in me to any attempt to change how I acted in the world. Even those who seem totally at ease in normal social settings often fear the judgments that society periodically renders on the very sensitive. I have a number of students who are very successful in the world and seem to be totally at ease around just about everybody. Even though they are far more socially adept than I will ever be, when we are exploring their inner selves together, they nevertheless cannot any longer hide the basic fear of the world with which they are afflicted.

The Fear of Nonseparateness

Perhaps a fear of the world and all its difficulties and judgments is at the core of everyone. Of course, this is not true of those totally amoral beings for whom other people exist only to be used (or if it is true, it is true in a very different way). I mean it is true for all those basically good people who are trying to figure out who they are and just what they are doing here.

The point is that as long as we behave as separate, discrete entities with clearly delineated boundaries who busily defend our personal space including our psyches, then easing those boundaries will be quite a challenge.

That is why, when we try to think of ourselves as beings of light, we feel a sense of danger. Our boundaries seem to become diffuse; there is no longer enough skin to separate us from others; there are only not-very-clearly-defined rays of light that all too easily mingle with our own rays of light. Often, as we sit in meditation with other people working on light practices like those I have described above, we realize suddenly that everybody around us is doing exactly the same thing; we realize that everybody is commingling with everybody else, that we are no longer separated by absolute boundaries—and we become very daunted, very uncertain, because we have been counting on those boundaries all along to guard our personal secrets and to maintain our sense of uniqueness as an individual.

However, if we are able to allow ourselves to accept the wisdom of the Sufis (and of other spiritual orders) and sink into the vast sea of individuals who are intermingled even while they know themselves to be separate individuals, then we will encounter one of the greatest treasures of life: the kinship of kindred spirits. You will discover that you have surrendered to an immense reality out of which your brothers and sisters support you, and not in competition, because you and they exist in and for one another. This realization contains the seeds of great power; were we all to have it, we would take giant strides toward healing the fundamental rift between us that the illusion of separation has created in all our societies.

As you pursue the spiritual path, you will notice that you have fleeting experiences of what I have described above—experiences that your ingrained defenses will make you instantly try to reject. One of the powerful defenses we have all erected around us is the one that protects us from being hustled in an unexpected manner. You think you sense a hustle or a con; you do not know what it is, but you are convinced there is one. Your basic experience has taught you that any new experience must be regarded with suspicion; and so it is that, when you sense your light-being commingling with the light-being of others, you naturally believe you smell a rat. "This feels too good to be good for me!" you exclaim, or, "Somehow—I haven't figured out how—I'm being hustled, and something bad is about to happen to me!"

This is a totally natural reaction; it is your psychic defenses automatically kicking up a fuss at an experience you do not understand yet. After all, you have worked hard at becoming a discrete entity, and all of a sudden your inner being is asking you to lay aside all that hard-won armor and become (or recognize that you already are) a crystalline structure of light! That is a lot to ask.

Be gentle with yourself as you go through this. If you have a spiritual guide, continually check in with the guide to have your progress monitored.

THE YEARNING SWITCH

We are back to the subject of willing surrender, which comes when the yearning for the Beloved has become so overwhelming that nothing else can quench the fire of the love we feel. Our need to merge with the ocean of union overrides all other needs and desires and becomes the only thing possible for the lovers we are.

You will have come across the sentiment I have just expressed if you have read the poetry of the Sufi saint Rumi. In fact, that feeling pervades all the ecstatic literature that Sufism has created over the centuries.

If you wish to share in that yearning, you have to ask yourself, "How do I turn on the Yearning Switch?" It is a good question. It is one I asked myself for years. And then, one day, my Yearning Switch turned on, all by itself—perhaps not as intensely as the rhapsodic paragraph above would tend to suggest, but it was definitely on. Today, the pull within me toward union has become an imperative I cannot deny, nor do I want to. But how I managed to turn on the switch, I have no idea.

The longing for the Beloved is in every one of us. In one sense, it is the desire to return to the cosmic womb, to the source of all our being. That yearning runs closer to the surface for the mystically inclined than it does in the rest of us. But even the mystic must undergo a certain amount of training—and of untraining—to be able to access and eventually surrender to the yearning.

One of the themes of this book is that we can and should allow that yearning to manifest within us and take its place as part of our experience of existence. The Yearning Switch has lain within us unactivated all along; the difficulty lies not in constructing it—it has been there all the while—but in finding out where it is so we can turn it on. Just how do we find it? You might try putting your head on the floor and asking God where it is located. Make this a daily exercise; eventually, something will begin to unfold.

Ultimately, surrender is the renewal of the vow of service we took before we became incarnate. We are spiritual beings, paying a visit to this planet to experience, to manifest, to evolve. Before we came, we took a vow that once born we would fulfill our original, prebirth purpose. It will help us to do so if we can see this world as a place of learning; if we can surrender to our soul's desire to know itself and its Creator.

Now, put your head to the floor!

He is brave who courageously experiences all things; he is a coward who is afraid to take a step in a new direction; he is foolish who swims with the tides of fancy and pleasure; he is wise who experiences all things, yet keeps on the path that leads him to his destination.

—Hazrat Inayat Khan

6

GETTING ON
THE PATH

I was chatting with a friend the other day when he suddenly asked me, "What happens when you're pursuing the spiritual path and you actually get to a certain level of enlightenment?"

"Beats me," I said. "It probably means more work."

"I'm serious," he retorted. "What happens when you become a mystic?"

I looked at him. "You used to say you were one," I replied.

"Not anymore."

Then I understood. "You're saying your horizons have just expanded," I said.

"I guess that's it."

We went on to talk about the effect this abrupt expansion of his inner horizons was having on how he viewed the world. At any given point in our lives, we tend to think that what we know is what there is, subject to minor technical modifications, and my friend had just had this point of view radically adjusted. In other words, whatever our view of the universe may be, we tend to think of its boundaries as set in stone or at least carved in wood. We may pay lip service to the idea of expanding our consciousness; perhaps we admit there are people around us whose consciousnesses are more expanded than ours (though not by much!); we may even acknowledge that there are extraordinary beings in the Himalayas and other remote areas who are in touch with God-consciousness, the Universal Mind, or whatever. But when we are actually pressed to try to broaden these frontiers ourselves, we likely cry out, "I can't do that, and even if I could, I'm not sure I'd believe that was what was really going on!" And we leave it at that. Our mind does not want to believe that change can take place in our consciousness. The idea is too upsetting. That was the case with my friend whose horizons had just expanded. He had had this wonderful experience of a change in spiritual location, and it had left him confused. He had discovered there was more to everything than he thought there was—his consciousness of the world had been ratcheted up a notch and widened out—but he did not know how to deal with the "moreness" of things he was now experiencing. His family was not happy with him either. He had changed, and despite his best efforts not to change, he was acting differently—and even spiritually sophisticated families have a hard time accepting aberrant behavior among their own and get confused when it happens.

We do our meditations; we read spiritual books and grapple with their ideas; we attend lectures and seminars given by people we admire and respect—we do all these things, and still, when the time of transformation comes, we are caught by surprise. It is one of the most fascinating aspects of this whole spiritual process. Part of it, I believe, is our love of, or need for, ritual. Whatever station we are presently at—a station (or *Maqaam*, in Sufi terms) being our level of realization or spiritual awareness—we tend to erect ritual around it. It could be the way we dress or how we walk or use body language, probably a combination of them. And, once a ritual is established, even if it is only two weeks old, we assume it has permanence.

Another factor may be that once we have gone through one of these transformations, we may not be at all eager to repeat the experience. It is, after all, pretty exhausting. All of that change and new ritual creation does take a toll.

MEMORY AND PERSISTENCE

What attitude should we take in the face of the stumbling blocks, in particular the ones I have just cited, that we meet along the way?

Pir Vilayat always had the same answer. He told us we must always push through, push through our doubt, push through our fear, even push through our elation. I liked the directness of that approach—though personally I also like sneaky, as in not letting your psyche know what you are planning to do. I like what my guide says, and that is simply, "Remember." This is so simple it took me a long time to figure out what she really meant. I finally realized she was saying, in effect, "Remember who you are when you are stretched out to the limits of your capabilities—the limits of which even you cannot know."

I believe memory is the key. At difficult junctures, we need to summon memories of past spiritual accomplishments: of fine meditations performed as flawlessly as can be; of personal retreats where we attained something unexpected; of the current of love that can pass between friends while in meditation. All these memories, and many others besides, create a core of memory that can sweep us up and carry us through the trauma of a change of station, a change of Maqaam, and support us as

85

we create new rituals that will sustain us until we arrive at the next level.

It is a misnomer to speak in spiritual circles of being "on the path"—though this misnaming is convenient. Our entire experience of life from birth to death is of a being on the path. Life itself is a journey, and everyone, whatever his or her spiritual status, is on that path; whether we have awakened to the knowledge of that journey is irrelevant.

What we in spiritual circles call "the path" might more properly be called "the response" or "the reflex." Something—let's say it is the soul's desire to know itself—wells up from deep inside us, and we respond. Since in most cases the call comes in a voice or style that is unfamiliar, we tend to respond inappropriately. One of the most common inappropriate responses is the belief that what has just happened to us is more important than it really is. Which is not to say it is not important; it is, because it is happening to us, and we are the most important person in our universe.

But try to keep things in perspective. Here is a basic rule:

If you can reproduce the experience anytime you want, that is a good thing. But if it happens once and you cannot reproduce it—well, that is fine, but do not take that particular experience too seriously.

Pir Vilayat had a wonderful line that always brought us all back to earth. It was: "You're chosen not because you're the best, but because you're the best available." In other words, some master or angel—whoever manages these affairs—has looked at the available talent and decided that the best he or she can come up with is you. I personally find this idea heartening. I am not expected to be Mahatma Gandhi, just me. You may also experience feelings of awe, terror, elation, ecstasy, remorse, and the absolute conviction that you have gone insane. All of these reactions, and others like them, are responses to an inner process that is really very natural.

We in the West have little feeling for the naturalness of the phenomena that stem from the spirit. We want to label what is happening. We want to compartmentalize it. We want to fit it into the Western scheme of things. We think of such experiences in two ways: (1) "They" are evil and want to eat us alive; or (2) "They" are holy and will save our souls. Aliens in science fiction stories usually fall into one or the other of these two categories, thus reflecting our society's tendency to think that something out of the ordinary is either an invasion of merciless beings or the advent of a new Jesus Christ.

Rarely does it occur to us to see something unusual and unknown simply as something that has not yet been defined. If we can stay with the feeling that something strange that has happened to us is simply something we do not know about, we are ready for the next step: doing something about this new experience.

WHEN THE CALL COMES

So, what do you do when the insistent call comes? Run to your priest or rabbi? That might work, but unless these individuals are schooled in mysticism and know what to do when, say, your kundalini—that core of psychic energy that is coiled up at the base of your spine just waiting to be released—opens, they are not going to be a lot of help. I will grant you that the number of professional priests who are trained in mysticism is increasing, and maybe you are lucky enough to have one. If so, he or she will certainly be able to tell you what to do.

How about seeking out a therapist, as that is the commonly accepted thing to do when a person is experiencing something

outside the norm? Again, it might work, if the therapist under-
stands spirituality.

Talk it out with your mom or dad or best friend? Maybe
you will get lucky; but more often than not, you will be worse
off than before because, as a rule—not always—your family and
friends will not want you to be anybody other than the person
they rely on to reflect their own natures and values. And if that
is sad, it is also true.

Find a teacher? There are a zillion of them out there, just
waiting to sell you crystals, meditation tapes, biofeedback ma-
chines, and so forth—but very few of them have a clue about
what constitutes spiritual practice. Some may be sincere, but
they may not have much on the ball. They can be sufficiently
bright, however, to take you for all your money—and what does
it say about you if you let them do this?

I am not being totally fair. You can look upon all these people vying for your spirituality dollars as part of the spiritual de-
velopment of our planet. If you want to spend your money that
way, go ahead. But once you have gone beyond what I call the
Unicorn Phase of spirituality—dealing with eccentric people
and practices—you will need a legitimate teacher who knows
what he or she is doing and whose concern is not an increase
in his or her bank account or personal power but your spiritual
progress. You will not get far on the path without a genuine
teacher. All the prophets were blessed with such a teacher (just
check the history books), and so were all the masters. I tried to
do without a teacher for years. The idea of putting myself under somebody else's thumb really bothered me. I read books on
spirituality. I pretended to meditate. I told everyone how cool
I was. But it was not until I met Pir Vilayat and asked him to
be my teacher that things began to fall into place for me. I will

not belabor the point, except to say that every esoteric tradition accepts that a teacher is essential for spiritual progress.

How do you find such a teacher, once the call from within has come?

Be patient. Recognize that you do not know yourself as well as you thought you did. Otherwise, you would have known that that inner voice existed. Patience is a supreme virtue here. Know that the teacher will come. The classic formulation for this is that for every step the student takes toward the teacher, the teacher takes ten steps toward the student. But patience has a downside. You have begun to glow from within—and the beacon of your internal flame is beginning to draw to you every spiritual wacko within a thousand miles. Your real teacher will not arrive at your door immediately and say, "Let's go!" First of all, you will have to work your way through this wave of wacko; it is as if your future teacher were hanging out there in some spiritual dimension waiting for you to learn discrimination.

You still have to seek out your teacher yourself, even though your teacher is drawing you to him or her. It is a joint responsibility. Be patient. Have your purpose clearly in your mind. Be calm. Then the person you seek will come. Let's say you have found a real teacher. You think you resonate with this person, and you say, "I want to be your student. Please initiate me."

And the teacher says, "No."

You have two options here. You can stomp off in a huff, convinced that the teacher made a mistake and that one day you will show this teacher where to get off.

Or you can insist.

If you stomp off in a huff, the teacher was right to refuse you.

If you insist, and the teacher finally says okay, the teacher was checking you out.

But if, despite all your insisting, the teacher still says no, you need to find out why. Generally there are two reasons. The first is that you approached a teacher of the wrong spiritual persuasion as far as your own growth is concerned; you needed, say, a Buddhist, and you encountered, say, a teacher of Vedanta.

The second reason is that what you really need is a therapist. Generally, though not always, the teacher will tell you why you have been refused. Be prepared to do some research into the differences among the various disciplines.

Teachers can be quite uncanny when it comes to figuring out who should be their students. I knew a woman who repeatedly asked one of Pir Vilayat's sheikhs to initiate her. He kept refusing until finally he told her he would initiate her on one condition, that she cleaned up her apartment. I do not know how he knew her apartment was a mess, but this was the condition he imposed.

Weeks, then months, went by, and she still had not cleaned up her apartment. A group of female Sufis finally came by to help her. But even as she thanked them profusely for coming, she blocked every effort they made to help her clean up her apartment. To the best of my knowledge, she still has not been initiated. What she really needed was a therapist. Also to the best of my knowledge, she still has not seen a therapist. I hope that she has cleaned up her apartment. Am I upsetting you by mentioning therapy? Just because you have received the call does not mean you are stable. Certainly, I was not. The recruiting angel apparently does not care about emotional stability. Nevertheless, esoteric work does absolutely require emotional stability. It is a mystery to me why the recruiting angel is not hip to this, but that is the way it is. If the teacher says, "Go get some therapy, then come back and see me"—do it. If the teacher says, "I really think your path is with this Ute shaman who lives in Santa Fe," go see that Ute shaman. In the final analysis, it's okay. We all belong to the same family.

Once you have been accepted by a teacher, say thank you and do what the teacher says. Do not ask the teacher to reorganize your life; do not ask the teacher to fix your finances; do not ask the teacher to talk to your boyfriend or girlfriend whenever you two have an argument.

What is your teacher's job? It is to give spiritual advice. In Sufism, there are two distinct schools of thought about the relationship between sheikh and mureed/student. One school of thought holds that the sheikh should know everything there is to know about the mureed, while the other maintains that a certain detachment should reign between sheikh and mureed. The debate has been going on for millennia, and it will probably never be resolved, especially as the approach that is adopted is very much a function of the teacher's personality. My wife and I know quite a lot about the lives of our students, but when it comes to issues of a personal nature, we strive for absolute neutrality. We try to follow Pir Vilayat's dictum of never giving personal advice. This works for us.

When you embark on the Sufi path, you are usually given basic instruction and one or two personal practices. Then the real work begins, that of keeping your mind on the training and actually doing the meditations you have been assigned. At first, this may seem relatively easy. And, in a way, it is. Normally you are simply asked to do practices that take up no more than fifteen or twenty minutes of your day; generally you are asked to do these in the morning. Often these beginners' practices consist of the repetition of a single Hindi or Sanskrit or Arabic word or set of words. This may seem odd at first, but you will get used to it, and it is not really all that difficult.

Here is the problem: the practices actually work. Your personality begins to change. This can be annoying, because the change is so subtle that you scarcely notice it—until the day comes when you find a good excuse for skipping meditation, and then you find a good excuse for skipping the next meditation, and then the next. . . . This is the first hint you have that your personality is rebelling; the practices have been acting on you very subtly, and your personality has been reacting just as subtly to try to remove these annoying influences from your life.

Paths of Love and Service

In Sufism we distinguish between the path of love and the path of service.

It took me a long time to understand the difference between these two paths of spirituality. In the beginning, I could not understand why some people melted at the sight of Pir Vilayat, sitting in rapt attention through his talks and at the end not being able to remember a single word he had said. To be truthful, I still have not quite figured this out. At the time, I pored over explanations in books, saying to myself, "Oh, so that's why! They are on the path of love, and devotion to the teacher is the primary focus. Later this can change to devotion to God!" But I still did not really understand. Now, however, I can see that there are people who are drawn to a particular spiritual order because of the leader's charisma. These are the people who pursue the path of love. At the same time, there is a smaller number of people who are drawn to a particular order because they have realized that this is where they will be able to carry on the work of serving—serving people, serving the community, serving God—that they know is their purpose in life. Both paths are equally valid; the first is the path of love and the second is the path of service.

There is no particular merit in being on one path as opposed to the other. The right path is the one you are suited for; it suits you, and it feels right, and that is all the reason you need. If being on the path begins to feel wrong, you should get off and go back to what you were doing before. Many do, and this is fine. Remember, though, that the discomfort you may be experiencing stems from the protests of your ego at the journey. If that is the case, this is something you have to work on. I have known people who have never had a moment's doubt about the rightness of the path they are on—but I have not known many people like that, and sometimes I have had my doubts about how they really felt. The student who questions and doubts all the time is far more common; doubting and questioning is as much a part of the spiritual path as paying attention to your meditation.

THE NEED FOR TRANSMISSION

A final word about why there is so much insistence on having a teacher and joining a group. That word is *transmission*. There is a certain amount of information and experience that the student can receive only by sitting in front of someone who has already received that information and experience, and who then transmits it to the student. This may sound like hocus-pocus, but it actually works.

Furthermore, you need a teacher because you do not really know where you are going or how you are going to get there. Pir-o-Murshid Hazrat Inayat Khan, Pir Vilayat's father and the founder of our Order, put it this way: "One may attain the purpose of life without a personal guide, but to try to do so is to be like a ship traversing the ocean without a compass. To take initiation, then, means entrusting oneself in regard to spiritual matters to a spiritual guide."

In other words: you might make it across the ocean without a compass, but you probably would not—so why try? A third reason why you need a teacher—and you will have to trust me on this one—is that in a spiritual order the student and the teacher establish a kind of magical connection that exists nowhere else except in this kind of relationship. This is a completely unique way for two human beings to be together, and once you have experienced it, you will be very reluctant to let it go. Additionally, you connect with the line of transmission that flows through the ages. This may be even more important than the individual connection.

But finally, you are the one who is responsible for yourself. If you choose to go off on your own, then so be it. If you decide that your path really lies in working on your career, and you want to save the spiritual stuff for later, then that is what works for you. Your decisions are what shape your life; they *are* your life, and they are your responsibility alone. But to receive the call to spirituality is a great blessing, and in my opinion it is a great shame not to respond to such a call.

If you do respond, the blessing will go on and on, in ways you cannot foresee but that you will never regret.

The whole Cosmos moves as a pendulum: the past and the future, transciency and eternity, human and Divine. It is out of the ever-constant back-and-forth dialogue between these two poles that the future is created. I believe that the future is not just something waiting for us; it is something that is built by sorting through the past for that which belongs to tomorrow; it is a continual work-in-progress that takes place in every era and that occurs through each individual's innovative, imaginative, and conscious participation. It is what I call spiritual evolution.

—Pir Vilayat Inayat Khan

7

BACK TO THE FUTURE

When Majida and I got married, the sheikh who performed the ceremony said, "The most remarkable thing about your relationship is that you two actually found each other."

I took that to mean that maybe there is no foolproof predestination scheme operating in the universe—that maybe there is a degree of randomness. When I combine the idea that none of us has one set future with the Sufi concept that all past, present, and future events exist "now" in the ocean of being of Wahdat Al Wujud, I have to conclude that we all have "memories" not just of one but of many possible futures. These are potential memories; some have more potential than others, but all are nonetheless merely the future in potential. I believe it is the presence of these potential future memories that gives rise to the experience in our lives that we normally call déjà vu.

Hazrat Inayat Khan once said that the dream world has the same reality as this one. It is only because we are so involved in this world and think we are cut off from the other, he said, that we do not believe the other world has the same validity. The Pir went on to say that what Sufism calls the Djinn world, and what it calls the Angelic world, also have the same validity as this world, and that we are cut off from them essentially because we are asleep to those worlds. He added that it is only the mystic who awakens to these worlds, and this as he gains in skill and inspired vision.

What Hazrat Inayat Khan said about the equi-validity of all realities seems to suggest that, while déjà vu is an interesting peculiarity of existence on our waking plane of time-space reality, it is a constant and common staple of the awareness of the true mystic, and probably a very helpful one (although it occurs to me that a never-ending hail of déjà vus in your life could be rather annoying).

Once, when Majida and I were in India managing a tour group for Pir Vilayat, we were fortunate enough to be invited to a session with Baba Sita Ram Das Onkarnath (who has since passed, but who at the time was regarded as one of the greatest living saints of India). Baba spoke only Gujarati, but he had an able translator. After about half an hour of instructing us, the great man had to stop, protesting that the astral plane was so noisy he was having great difficulty concentrating on this plane of existence. Pir Vilayat later told me that Baba's aura was so bright he almost could not look at him (I guess there is a downside to everything).

THE ARROW OF TIME

Pir Vilayat had an exercise that he offered to help the students find their way through the psychic minefield represented by all those other planes of existence, having the same reality as ours, that are constantly impinging upon us but of which we are not—usually—consciously aware. He called this exercise the

Arrow of Time, and it operated on the principle that the pull of the future is stronger than the push of the past—that the being that you are becoming draws you to find the path to its fulfillment.

Pir Vilayat writes in *Awakening: A Sufi Experience*:

The Sufis have developed a metaphysics of time and fate dramatically different from the ordinary, linear perception of time. For instance, they distinguish between the moment when the past overlaps the future in a way that inevitably shapes it, and a simultaneously occurring instant when the forward-moving arrow of time is intersected by a transcendent dimension—like an infusion of fresh, uncreated energy into circumstances that have become fixed and stagnant.

But to focus on only one part of this statement: it takes courage to believe that the being you are becoming draws you to find the path to its fulfillment. Why courage? Because the being you are becoming is so much greater than the puny self you imagine yourself to be. Looking at your future Self, at this far more complete and integrated Self you are becoming, can be an embarrassing and intimidating experience. It is the rare individual who can look at this Self that is coming, understand what is happening—and look upon all this as a promising experience!

This person you are looking at, your future Self, is essentially a stranger. Spiritual teachers are constantly perplexed with the problem of how to convince students it is okay to move out of who they are into who they are becoming; that is why there are so many stories about a teacher's putting a student through a trial that inevitably leads to a psychic shock. The teacher must be both astute at recognizing when the student is ready for the shock and creative in the application of that shock. I used to say to myself—after Pir Vilayat had nailed me several times with essential psychic shocks—what can the Pir do to me now that I will not recognize coming? My psyche had become wary and watchful. But, fortunately for me, Pir Vilayat never lost the capability of surprising me even when I knew that something was on the way.

THE DANGERS OF PRECOGNITION

I do not think that we can force the future to reveal its intent as far as the Self we are becoming is concerned (perhaps some of you out there know how to do this, but I am not aware of any exercises that can lead to this objective). All we can do is ride out the waves of information that come rolling in from the future. Please remember, if you can, that a precognitive capability—an ability to know the future beforehand—is a side effect, not a desired result. In fact, this ability can cause a lot of trouble, because almost no one will believe what you have seen, including yourself. Such skepticism is probably a good thing, since, as I have suggested above, all futures are potential, and we do not know which particular bits of precognition belong to our time-space world and which are a part of the vaster reaches of the multi-universes.

I know someone who has doom and disaster visions frequently. Usually, she will find herself in a place or a building and know—be absolutely certain!—that something very unpleasant is about to happen in that place or building. Generally she ignores these visions of doom, thinking them to be a manifestation of her incipient claustrophobia (she has trouble being in confined spaces). But when something bad happens of which she has had a vision, then she remembers that she had that vision. She has told me that two days before the 1993

100

World Trade Center bombing, she dreamed she was there, in the World Trade Center, and that she felt terribly uncomfortable and urgently had to get out.

More frequently, my friend is aware of something unpleasant that is about to happen to a person. Sometimes she is aware of the impending death of that person. Obviously this is the kind of information that, when it comes surging through you, is hardly calculated to give you peace of mind. What my friend finds particularly confusing is that most of the things she sees do not happen. She has had to learn how to distinguish between the subtly different gradations of power of the various visions she receives. She can pretty much tell now when something is close to manifestation. But it has taken her years to sort all this out.

As is so often the case with aspects of spirituality, precognition is a very subtle phenomenon, hardly an in-your-face kind of a thing. That is why we do not even notice a great deal of the information we get. If we do notice something, we tend either to ignore it or to give it much more weight than it probably deserves. I am not speaking here of those genuine psychics who are very tuned in to the aspects of creation outside of time and space. They are an entirely different breed and have a whole other set of problems they must deal with. Rather, I am talking about those persons who, from time to time, look around and realize that they have been in this situation before—or they think they have. This probably happens to everyone, but, when you begin to recognize your spiritual sensitivity to this sort of thing, the awareness of that sort of information increases within you. Why? Because you are looking—sometimes desperately—for proof of that strange reality that seems to be overtaking you. And, when you look for that kind of knowledge, you will find it.

It is the soul's light which is natural intelligence.
—Hazrat Inayat Khan

8

AUTHENTICITY
AND
WATCHFULNESS

When I was a young man serving in the Army in Korea, I decided to join a skydiving club. I really had no idea what I was getting into, but the idea seemed glamorous and daring. I went through ground school, learning theory, how to fall, how to pack a parachute, and the myriad other things you need to know to be safe and enjoy yourself.

Then, after the required classes, I was permitted to go to the drop zone for my first jump. It was easy. All the sensations were so new and exciting that I did not have the sense to be scared; I was just completely thrilled. I made a second jump that day; then I was scared, but I did it anyway, overcoming my fear and continuing to make jumps. I made 120 jumps in all over a three-year period, which is not a lot by skydiving standards but was a lot for me, as jumps are expensive and I have never been one to have a surplus of disposable income. After awhile, I stopped.

Little did I know back then that some fifteen years later I would be listening to Pir Vilayat tell people they should do something dangerous in their lives, like skydiving or rock climbing, because it was important that you test your courage in certain basic ways. It was then that it occurred to me that skydiving and meditation are pretty similar in that in both of them you take a step into the unknown and put your life—or, worse still, in the case of meditation, your ego—on the line. In fact, both share three steps in all: some (usually) very heavy anticipatory worry; a plunge into the unknown; and a post-plunge assessment.

In some ways, skydiving's leap into the unknown is easier than the leap into the unknown of meditation. When you skydive, at least the jump is right there in front of you; you can see what you are doing, and all you have to do is decide whether to jump. On the other hand, in spiritual matters you usually cannot see where the edge of the cliff is, and you have no idea when to jump.

It is no exaggeration to say that bouts of worried anticipation appear at intervals along the spiritual path. I will tell you about a couple of my own that continue to pop up from time to time. First, there is the absolute conviction that my spiritual guide is seeing right through me and in the next moment will find out that I am completely worthless. A second is the sense that something awful is about to happen to me (though the feeling that nothing *at all* is going to happen to me—and never will—is almost as bad).

We often feel uncertain about how far along the spiritual path we are capable of going—that is, how high a skydive we have it in us to make. To deal with this fear (and the two I mentioned above), we need to keep in the forefront of our mind the thought that all the practices and all the meditations we do serve just two purposes:

- to reprogram our personality slowly and steadily
- to prepare us for the moment of transformation

When you are reprogramming the personality, you have to take into account the anticipatory nature of the ego. In meditation (as in skydiving), the ego protects itself against what is coming by creating a scenario—any scenario. But, being the ego and being just as clueless as the personality, it really has no idea what is coming, and you have to keep in mind constantly that the great raft of expectations it is putting forth are usually highly misleading.

We guides often hear the disgruntled question, "Why isn't anything happening? I've been doing this practice for three years, and nothing has happened yet." And even as the person is saying that, we guides are gazing into his or her face and observing that it is positively glowing with spiritual energy, even though the person obviously has no clue of this transformation that has been taking place within. It is as if we are protected from being arrogant while we are on the spiritual path by a personal lack of awareness as to how far we have really traveled. Let me illustrate.

A distinguished *sannyasi*, a Hindu holy man, whom Pir Vilayat knew from his travels in the Himalayas, tells this story about himself.

When this man decided to take the yellow robe, the garb of the mendicant spiritual seeker in the Hindu tradition, he was obliged to search out a place in which to do his meditations. Apparently one of the vows you take in this tradition is to choose a place of meditation and stay there whatever occurs. The sannyasi wanted to begin his practices far from civilization. In India this means being where there are predators. He searched for a long time until he found what seemed to be the perfect place: a beautiful valley with a good cave, water within walking distance, and an abundance of fruits and vegetables. There were no signs of predators. He took a formal vow to remain there till he found the Self. Just then the unmistakable cough of a tiger echoed through the forest. He knew he had made the wrong decision. The sannyasi hid in the cave for two days. On the third day he waited until midday, hoping the tiger would be holed up somewhere to avoid the heat. Then, no longer able to control his thirst, he rushed to the stream, filled his container, and turned back toward the cave.

The tiger stepped out on the path in front of him. The sannyasi's first impulse was to flee. But he knew that would be pointless. His next thought was to race for a nearby tree and climb it, thus to escape the tiger's claws. He could wait until the tiger was gone, then flee the valley forever. But what about the vow he had taken not to leave the valley until he had found enlightenment? If he broke his vow, how could he ever expiate this sin? He truly did not know what to do. He was terrified of the tiger and wanted to flee, but he was equally appalled at the idea of breaking his vow. Then a calm descended on him. He decided that he had taken a vow and that, whatever the outcome, he would see that vow through to the end. If God had decided he would best serve humanity by being eaten by a tiger, then so be it. Having made his decision and having overcome his terror, he stood his ground and watched calmly as the tiger approached.

The tiger padded up him. Slowly, it rubbed its long powerful body up and down the sannyasi's thigh. Then it escorted him back to the cave.

Thereafter, until he attained enlightenment, the sannyasi shared the valley with the tiger.

Getting Away from Backing Off

You can see that the personality of the sannyasi had no idea what was going on, while his spirit knew enough to wait quietly and simply to accept whatever happened. Taking a vow is a serious thing, and mysticism is full of stories about what happens to initiates when they "take hands," as we say—make a vow. But it is here that the experience of the skydiver begins to separate itself from the experience of the initiate. The skydiver usually floats quietly to the ground. The initiate usually gets to watch his or her life fall apart while having the pleasure of participating in that collapse.

If your intention has been serious, this collapse is merely appearance. What is actually happening is that who you really are is emerging and confronting who you think you are, with all the unenlightened notions of the latter. This is a messy business, since we are usually very attached to who we think we are and will defend to the death that version of ourselves and everything it stands for.

To maintain your balance during this difficult time, you need to be in a constant state of watchfulness. Let us suppose that after a great deal of hard work and introspection you actually find yourself poised at the edge of this dangerous if metaphorical abyss. You gaze into its depths, and you say, "No way." You back off, abandoning all the hard work you have done to make it to the edge of this abyss. You will do this backing off many times. I have done this backing off many times myself. It took me fifteen years just to realize that this was what I was doing, and another ten years to figure out what to do about it.

What to do about it turned out to be very hard and very simple at the same time. A great deal of how we see ourselves is wrapped up in how we think others see us, and we spend a great deal of our time conducting ourselves in such a way that those views of others (or what we think those views are) continues to be correct. When we begin to take responsibility for our actions, one of the most important things to pay attention to is who we really are as opposed to who other people think we are. That is fairly simple to grasp. The harder part is continuously paying attention and catching all the moments when we forget that we are personally responsible for our own beings.

After you work your way through all this, however long it takes, and fight your way back to the edge—you jump. Or maybe you do not jump, for even at this point you can still back off and think about it for a time. Eventually, though, if you are to be true to your vow, you must take this plunge into the unknown.

It may well be, after you have taken the plunge, that when you turn around and look at where you leaped from, you discover that it was a two-foot fall and not the plunging abyss that you imagined—which is not to say that what you just did may not have been a profound and life-altering event.

Hazrat Inayat Khan writes:

It is only those who are blessed by perceiving the origin and source of all things, who awaken to the fact that the real inclination of every life is to attain to something which cannot be touched or comprehended or understood. The hidden blessing of this knowledge is the first step to perfection. Once awake to this fact, man sees there is something in life that will make him really happy and give him his heart's desire. He can say, "Though there are many things in life which I need for the moment and for which I shall certainly work, yet there is only that one thing, around which life centers, that will satisfy me: the spiritual attainment, the religious attainment, or, as one may even call it, the attainment of God."

Such a one has found the key to all happiness, and has found that all the things he needs will be reached because he has the key to all. "Seek, and ye shall find; knock, and it shall be opened unto you. Seek first the kingdom of God, and all these things shall be added unto you."

This kingdom of God is the silent life: the life inseparable, eternal, self-sufficient and all-powerful. This is the life of the wise, whatever be the name given to it; this is the life which the wise contemplate. It is the face of this life that they long to see; it is the ocean of this life that they long to swim in. As it is written, "In Him we live and have our being."

HONORING THE TRUE SELF

The deeper we delve into spirituality, the more we are forced to constantly examine what we do and the more we become aware of inappropriate thoughts and behavior. No one else need know about these objects of embarrassment that we increasingly come across. But we know. As I have already mentioned, this profoundly embarrassing and profoundly necessary examination of what we do is called, in Sufism, Muhasaba.

In carrying out this continuous examination, you honor the true Self. Your inner Self does not need reasons to exist. It wants spiritual freedom, and it is up to who you think you are—i.e., the external personality or ego—to provide it. To honor the true Self is simple: all you need do is admit that you yourself, as the personality, do not know what the Self needs—but that something inside you does know and that this is the Self that ultimately controls your life. The experience of this inner Self is glory and its being is innocence, and it exists in each and every one of us. Pir Vilayat says that Sufis are the ambassadors of God. Certainly, then, our assessment of what constitutes our true Self—and what constitutes our true position in the "spiritual hierarchy"—has to be accurate. This is something about which it is difficult to be objective, and that is why we need a guide. Here is a story that will illustrate my point:

A thousand years or so ago, a sultan was extremely fond of a certain Sufi sheikh. So enamored was he of this sheikh that he asked the sheikh if he could become his mureed. "No," replied the sheikh. "You are not ready."

The sultan was very upset by this rejection. He lobbied the sheikh's mureeds to try to persuade the sheikh to accept him as a mureed. The mureeds did as the sultan asked. The sheikh finally relented to the extent that he told the sultan that he could come live in the Tekah, the Sufi community house, but that he would not give him initiation and, moreover, that the sultan would have to do whatever the sheikh asked. The sultan readily agreed. He thought that in living near the sheikh he would be able to convince him of his own wonderful qualities and thus hasten the day of his initiation. The sultan was pleased with this arrangement—until he found out what duties the sheikh had in store for him. He would be the kitchen scull, the lowest of the low, cleaning the greasiest of the pots, taking the garbage out, and performing every other kind of manual labor.

The sultan had never done anything like this before. But he was determined to succeed and become a mureed, and so he decided to persevere and do the best he could. All went well for a month as the sultan resolutely went about his duties that were certainly not a part of his normal routine as the ruler of this country.

Observing all this, the mureeds began to sympathize with the sultan. They approached the sheikh and pleaded the sultan's case, pointing out that he was faithfully carrying out all the duties assigned to him and should now be considered for initiation.

But again came the sheikh's reply, "He is not ready." The mureeds were stunned. They continued to plead the sultan's case until finally the sheikh said, "I'll prove to you that he's not ready."

The sheikh arranged for a demonstration. He and the mureeds waited in a place where they could not be observed for the time when the sultan would take the kitchen garbage to the town dump. As soon as the sultan came out of the Tekah with the garbage, the sheikh had a young boy dart out into the street and collide with him, knocking him over and making the garbage scatter all over the street. The sultan jumped up and screamed every sort of invective at the boy. Then he gathered up his garbage and, grumbling all the while, continued on his way to the dump.

The sheikh gave the watching mureeds an "I told you so" stare and went back to his rooms.

Another month went by. Again the mureeds pleaded the sultan's case. Again the sheikh replied that the sultan was not ready. He even arranged the same demonstration as before, to which the sultan responded in the same manner—except that this time the sultan did not scream at the boy but merely muttered curses under his breath as he picked up the garbage.

A third month passed. The mureeds approached the sheikh once again. Sighing, the sheikh arranged another demonstration. This time when the sultan left the Tekah and the boy darted out into the street and knocked him over, the sultan simply picked up the garbage with no expression on his face and with a demeanor that said, "I have this task to complete."

This time the sheikh turned to the watching mureeds, smiled, and said, "Now he is ready."

As far as I know this is a true story. The sheikh was Sheikh Abul Fazl Fusail Bin Ayaz, and the sultan was Sultan Ibrahim Adham Al Balkhi; these two represent the fourth and fifth sheikhs on our silsila, our silsila being the list of sheikhs and pirs in our Order from Hazrat Khwaja Ali, the nephew of Muhammad, down to the present day. For years I watched people get upset because they thought they were ready for something, and the Pir thought they were not. For a long time I thought getting upset like this was a peculiarly American phenomenon. But after hearing the story I recounted above and reading many accounts of the lives of ancient Sufis, I have come to the realization that this kind of spiritual standoff has been around in many different places and for a very long while. I have realized that, as painful as we may find it, we really do need to accept the assessment of the individual with whom we seek to entrust our spiritual life. Which is not to say that we should just accept blindly. Not at all. It is much better to pay attention to what is being said to us, to examine our own reactions and see what happens. Sufism is not a path of utter devotion to the teacher, regardless of what that teacher may say. It is instead a path of self-discovery created by the student, not the teacher.

Exercise 9: Avoiding Gossip

Here is an exercise. It seems simple, but it will try you to the very limits of your soul (my students know this and groan whenever I assign it). It is simply this:

Avoid all gossip for one week.

If you think this is too easy for you, take it a step further and for one week do not talk about anybody who is not in the same room with you.

You have my guarantee that you will realize great benefits from this exercise!

THE OPENING OF THE HEART

When I first became part of the Sufi Order, I was puzzled for a very long time by the statement that Sufism is the path of the heart. It made no sense to me. I was equally puzzled by the statement that we must continually strive to open our heart.

Open your heart: that sounded good to me, but how did you do it? I did not want to appear like a dummy, so I never asked anybody exactly how to do it—a guy thing, I suppose—but just kept on doing the practices I was given, thinking that if ever I did get an open heart (whatever that was) probably I would know it. I suppose I thought this event of the opening of my heart would be accompanied by fireworks and maybe dancing girls—chaste ones, of course—and much rejoicing in heaven and lots of other nifty happenings that would let everyone know that I now had an open heart. Well, I waited, and I waited—and nothing happened. I kept on doing my practices and going on personal retreats and absorbing other experiences as they came my way, but this open-heart stuff continued to elude me.

After a while, I just stopped thinking about it and concentrated on other things.

What I had not taken into account was the subtlety of what we in the Order do. I thought I understood it, but I did not, not really. Usually at the end of a retreat Pir Vilayat would say something to us like, "We have talked a lot about the inexplicable," or, "Words are totally inadequate to describe this," or

113

words to that effect. I can well remember the first time I heard him express this thought, and the smug "Well, of course" I felt at the time. But I did not really understand. And, as the years went by, I began to understand that he was telling the simple truth. Words indicate, point, perhaps give clues, but they cannot actually describe experience. So the phrase "opening of the heart" that I was trying to understand with my mind kept eluding me.

And then it happened.

I was taking a personal retreat when it happened—the opening of my heart, I mean. Actually, it had been happening all along; I just had not noticed it. My retreat guide had given me a very difficult practice, and I was having a lot of trouble getting it, and day after day she kept giving it to me again. I was determined to master it, if only to move on to something else—when all of a sudden I had this very clear image of a sun in my heart, shining a brilliant golden orange and radiating out from my chest and back. At the same time there was a second image: that of the "white hole" that the Pir speaks of as being in the center of our being.

But did I care about any of this? Nope; all I cared about was learning how to do this annoying practice. So I sat there in the retreat room shining like the sun and ignoring it because it was not nearly as important as what I was doing. After the retreat was over, I still had not mastered that practice to my satisfaction. But I noticed that this glowing heart seemed still to be hanging around. I was relieved to discover that no one else could see it, but at the same time I was a little disappointed; it had occurred to me that I might finally have gotten one of those open hearts, but it was not nearly as spectacular an event as I had expected, so I was not quite sure. Anyway, the glow lasted for about a month and then gradually faded so that the day came when I was not aware of it anymore. While it was still there, though, I would look down at it from time to time and wonder what I was supposed to do about it. I never did come up with an answer. Such was my experience, and you are probably wondering why I even bothered to tell you about it. My point is that my inability to recognize what had happened to me was probably just another guy thing: I had already acquired an open heart, but I could not admit it to myself, because this very valid experience of mine was clothed in such a—to me—hokey description. I have always been able to feel people intensely and to know their truth—which is no big deal; it is what I do—but I could not accept this particular terminology. So I guess God gave me this experience, or maybe I somehow invented it for myself, to show me how silly it was to reject out of hand an experience just because it was clothed in a certain description that might not sound manly to my ears. Over the years, I have seen many people get hung up on definitions and phraseology while ignoring the truth behind the definition and the implications of that truth.

THE UNIMPORTANCE OF EXPERIENCE

A word about telling other people about your experiences:

You may tell your guide about your experiences, but no one else. The reason for this is that you want to avoid comparing your own experiences with those of others and finding fault with your own as well as theirs.

Let me put it as simply as possible: experiences do not mean much. There is a story about a student named Shamcher Bourse who was initiated into the Order by Hazrat Inayat Khan and for a time served as his translator and secretary. Shamcher had risen to the title of murshid, but once when he was asked about the kinds of spiritual experiences he had had, he merely replied that he had faithfully done his meditations and practiced *Dhikr* (Remembrance of God) for forty years, and that during that whole period he had never had a single "experience." "But," he concluded, "Dhikr made me what I am today."

(Dhikr, or *Zikr*, as it is sometimes spelled, is the basic practice of Sufism. The word literally means "to remember" and points to the central purpose of Sufism as a remembering of ourselves and our place in the universe. The practice consists of the repetition of a sacred word or phrase. The most often repeated phrase is Arabic, *La Ilaha Illah 'llah*, which means "Nothing Exists Except God.")

We tend to think of spiritual experiences as a sort of payoff for hard work or at the very least as a little bit of recognition for our efforts. If it appears that somebody else is getting a better payoff than we are, then—well, you know where that can lead, and so you can see that such a path leads in absolutely the wrong direction.

NONINTENTIONALITY: EXPECTING NOTHING

This brings me to the important subject of intention. I have already said that there is no compulsion in Sufism. But I have also said that there *is* compulsion in Sufism, in that you have no choice. This is a paradox with which the student of Sufism has to come to terms at some point. You practice Sufism because you have to—but you do not have to. I once asked one of our sheikhs if he ever thought of quitting the Order. "Sure," he replied. "But where would I go?" And that pretty much sums it up. As annoying and frustrating as it can be to pursue this path, you cannot imagine yourself doing anything else. And, if it is true that you are both compelled and not compelled, then you truly have no choice but to do the best work that you can.

This means paying attention to your motives. You will recall that earlier in this chapter I defined the practice of Muhasaba as continuously asking yourself: "What am I doing?" So ask. Look at how you are doing your meditations and see if you can decipher your motives. Are you simply going through the motions and fulfilling some sort of duty? Are you expecting a payoff? Both of these are pretty normal motives for proceeding; they have been mine, and they will be yours.

For example, when you have been doing *Quddus* (Quddus means Holy Spirit, and the implication is that you have been trying to bring yourself into alignment with the spirit of God), it is hard to avoid thoughts like, "So, when do I get to see the Holy Spirit? I mean, come on, I've been calling out your name for six months now, and you still haven't put in an appearance. Is that really fair?" But your motive should not be to call forth the Holy Spirit. You should not be expecting anything at all.

You want your intention to be as pure as possible. This requires work, just like anything else. As soon as an expectation or an opinion is layered onto a practice, that practice loses its effectiveness. Chanting for personal wealth is probably not a Sufi reason for chanting.

Let me refine the notion of intention further. I would say that it is best defined as controlled surrender. You have a feeling, perhaps vague, that there is something to aspire to that is greater than yourself—but what that something is, is quite unclear. Nevertheless, the power of this feeling compels you to do something. You must hold onto that feeling as the prime motivator—you must not allow it to sidetrack you into an emotional dead-end—and if you do manage to hold onto it in that way, you will find that you are able slowly to surrender further to that feeling. The important thing is not to get too excited about what effect this might have on you. There is a multitude of stories about mureeds who did their practices for fifty years and never felt a thing—but became the most beloved person in the village. You may not feel anything, but other people surely will; just be careful not to ask them what effect you are having.

As you can see, intention can be a fairly complicated business, because you are continuously having to examine yourself for selfishness. Actually, Sufism has no problem with selfishness, believe it or not, because it requires a certain selfishness to do what we do; it requires a certain paying attention to the Self to the exclusion of all else. What Sufism does have a problem with, however, is—let me see, what does the Pir call it? Oh, yes—concupiscence. You can look that one up. Think of it as your homework, figuring out where your concupiscence is and what you can do about it.

When the artist loses himself in his art,
then the art comes to life.
—Hazrat Inayat Khan

9

CREATIVITY:
WALK LIKE A KING

As a woodworker, I love few things better than lathe work—
"turning" a beautiful chunk of wood into a beautiful bowl
or other round object.

But lathe work is the most difficult and frustrating of all the
woodworking skills. I have been turning for ten years now, and
I have only just begun to feel I can truly create something beautiful when I practice my skill.

I still approach a valuable piece of wood with hesitation. It
is not that I am worried about the price of the material, which
can easily run you $100 a pound for a piece of rare walnut
burl. It is rather that I hesitate to violate the potential of a
unique and beautiful piece of virgin wood. For example, I have
a large piece of maple burl a friend gave me. Maple burl retails
at $5 a pound; my piece weighs at least fifty pounds. I turned
one bowl, and it came out nicely, but the rest of the piece sits
on my shop floor beside the lathe, waiting for my next burst of
courage. Even though this piece of burl was free, I do not want
to mess it up.

When I finally decide to toss a piece of wood on the lathe and have at it, something wonderful happens: the anxious "I" goes away, and I just create. Once you have made the decision to apply tool to material, the path is set. I am never totally sure what will come out of one of these woodworking sessions. All I know is that I have placed a piece of wood on the lathe and the end product will be bowl-like; beyond that, anything can happen. Usually I am innocent of intent. I believe true creativity requires this innocence of intent. You create for creation alone and not for anything you might get out of it beyond the process of creating, such as praise or money. I am not dismissing praise or money, but for our current purposes they are beside the point.

Neither am I saying that you do not need skill. When I fasten a piece of wood on the lathe, the skills I have assiduously acquired through the years kick in; simply wanting to create a beautiful object is not enough.

And I am certainly not saying that you should not pay close attention every instant. Did I mention that the lathe is the one woodworking tool that can kill? There are others that can eat your fingers off and even take away your arms, but if a twenty-pound chunk of wood comes flying off the lathe spinning at 1,000 rpm, you had better not be standing in the way.

But true creativity is something that comes from deep within you. It is at one and the same time a conscious and an unconscious process.

Such is also the case with the practices and meditations that come when you travel the spiritual path.

THREE KINDS OF SPIRITUAL CREATIVITY

There are three kinds of creativity in spirituality. The first is that of the artist; and, since the woodworker is or should be an artist, it is the kind of creativity that enables me to transform a beautiful piece of wood into a beautifully rounded object.

The second kind of creativity, closely allied to the first, is the kind of creativity that enables you to remold your personality, this being the basic hard work of spirituality that you find out has to be done once the process of awakening has begun within you.

Third, there is the kind of creativity that is the act of joining with the universe in the process of creation. This can be thought of as Self-realization, or doing what you do when you have finally arrived.

In all three, there is a powerful element of having to learn hard skills, but at the same time you have to forget all about that and simply be.

We encourage beginners on the spiritual path not to be too creative. We do this not because we consider beginners to be lacking in ability or potential, but because they do not have the requisite expertise and technical information. In spirituality, there are no twenty-pound chunks of wood that can come flying out at you and kill you. But doing something foolish in spirituality can mess you up for a time or send you down an inappropriate path. So it is best for you to pay attention to your guide and learn the rules before you try to break any of them. (Someone like Pir Vilayat is at the other end of the spectrum; he discovers the rules, such as they are, and when he comes back from a retreat and announces that he has discovered some new combinations, everyone grabs a notebook and listens hard. The rest of us—representatives and experienced students—lie somewhere in between these two extremes.)

Following the spiritual path does involve a lot of time. Maybe that is why ecstatic poetry like that written by the great Sufi poet Rumi is so popular: somehow the confrontation with our smaller self does not seem so bad because of the verbal beauty with which Rumi describes it. But in spirituality, as in everything worthwhile, patience is the key—patience, and the basic assurance of your own worth and of your capacity to effect meaningful change within yourself.

Exercise 10: Walk Like a King

Here is one of the core techniques of the art of creatively remolding yourself.

I want you to imagine yourself as the sovereign being you really are (this exercise is akin to Exercise 2, "Imagining the Master"). When you walk, walk like a king or a queen. When sovereigns walk, how do they view the world around them? I am talking about that royalty that takes full responsibility for all that it governs and that knows itself as the servant of all that it surveys, while at the same time knowing that it is due a certain deference.

In the United States, we have created an entire society based on the idea of littleness, in which the media's pervasive message is that we are flawed and can fix ourselves only by buying this toothpaste or that deoderant. But what if, instead, we were to regard one another as royalty? If I defer to your sovereign soul, and you defer to mine, this creative act will completely change how we think and feel about each other. First, though, you must glimpse the fundamental reality that you are a sovereign soul. Then you will know how you should see others, and how others should see you. So, walk like a king. Or like a queen.

Walk like a sovereign soul.

Knowing your sovereign soul for what it is: that is the first great creative act with which you will begin your journey along the spiritual path.

The next part of your spiritual training is the long, hard work of reprogramming your personality. You began with the act of visualizing your greatness. I am going to give you some exercises that will reinforce that. But first I need to tell you a bit more about what I mean by reprogramming the personality.

REPROGRAMMING THE PERSONALITY

Pir Vilayat was adamant in insisting that we never totally lose our personality or get away from our individual quirks. What we do as we move along the spiritual path, he said, was soften those quirks; we begin to see them in all their unreality, as no more than dream impressions. At the same time, we begin to honor them.

Our objective is not ego eradication. It is the realignment of the ego so that it assumes its proper place within the scheme of things. Our objective is certainly not allowing the ego to control all our actions. It is admitting that there are areas of inappropriate behavior within ourselves that need attention. There are surprises in store for us when we find these areas, many of which we cannot get to unless we change. Finally, it is admitting that what we really desire is union with the Beloved and that we will do whatever it takes to make this union happen.

When we are faced with all these warnings, admonitions, and hard work, our natural response is to deny that there is anything that needs to be changed. It is one thing to listen to the inner call; it is quite another to mess with something we have gone to such lengths to create, namely, our personality. And even while we politely agree that, yes, we see the necessity

125

of restructuring our personality, on an unconscious level we fight that decision tooth and nail.

Exercise 11: *Fana-fi*: Dissolution in the Being of Another

Here is another exercise that can help you and that can be done anytime. This practice is similar to Exercise 2, "Imagining the Master," and Exercise 10, "Walk Like a King." It is known as *fana-fi*. Fana-fi refers to the dissolution of the self in the being of another. For this exercise, imagine that you are sitting facing another human being—your spiritual guide, or, if you do not have a spiritual guide, a spiritual being you greatly admire.

Imagine you are sitting facing progressively greater spiritual beings.

The stages of greatness have names; you ascend the spiritual ladder from fana-fi Sheikh (the Teacher) to fana-fi Pir (a Persian word that literally means the Old One) to fana-fi Rasul (the Archetype of the Prophet) to fana-fi Allah (God).

You work through the same process at every stage. It is not an easy process. Imagine you are sitting in front of the guide you have chosen, visualizing that person in his or her highest state and totally accepting the being of that person. Once you have become comfortable with this process, superimpose the features of the guide on your own features; take the mantle of the guide's being and allow it to flow over and within your own being, as if you were becoming the being you are imagining. Next, assume the personality of the guide. Feel that you can react as that person reacts, feel as he or she feels. Finally, enter into the consciousness of the guide, of the highest level of spiritual awareness of the guide, and make it your own, or at least gain a deeper understanding of what that reality is. Then, move on to the next stage—but you must make sure you have firmly grasped one stage before you go on to the next.

There is another way of doing this practice. You can concentrate on an object rather than a person. Essentially, it is the same practice, without the added difficulty of the human personality. Choose an object you find beautiful. It can be a flower or an elegant piece of pottery or something of that sort, but its basic form must be simple; it should not be a complex arrangement of lines and colors, as in a painting. Let's take a rose, for example. First, look at the rose. Then close your eyes and see the rose in your mind's eye. Open your eyes and look at the rose again; then close your eyes and see the rose in your mind's eye once again. Continue to do this until the image in your mind's eye is solid enough that there is no drift or fading; hopefully, you will be able to do this naturally, without straining.

The next stage consists of imagining what it is like to be the rose. The stage after that consists in imagining roseness. The stage after that—the final stage—is one of imagining the essence of flowerness as it exists throughout the universe.

When I give this practice, I generally tell the students to do each stage for at least a month. If they have trouble moving up the ladder, I tell them to go back and start over again.

CHAPTER NINE

RESPONSIBILITY

Responsibility is another aspect of spirituality that falls into the category of creativity. (I have tried to avoid this topic, since no one ever likes to talk about it, but I am afraid the time has come to broach the subject.)

So far, I have talked about things like how you can know where you are on the path and how you can defend yourself against your own silliness—both are commonly encountered pitfalls as you travel the spiritual path, and there are many more of a similar stripe.

Over and above these pitfalls lies the necessity of the student's fostering a sense of responsibility to the spiritual hierarchy and to humankind. This sense of responsibility, while a driving force, is a secondary driving force; the primary driving force in what we do is love.

When I bring the subject of responsibility up in class, my students cringe; it is as if they are saying, "Can't we just stick with the easy stuff, like a nice simple seven-level meditation, and not do responsibility?" They react this way because taking responsibility implies doing something, and in this hectic day and age people do not want to add more things to their "to-do" lists. I am not saying people are irresponsible; I am saying that they find it difficult to think about responsibility. I was talking with a student the other day about her great desire to go to India. She had decided not to go because she felt her spiritual work was here in the United States, and that traveling to India would be like eating spiritual chocolates, tasty but not really nutritious—in fact, a rather selfish act. I understood. Going to India would have been a going-back to the past. A tradition of mysticism has to be built up here in the West, and those of us on the construction crews take our work very seriously. We need to create an entirely new mysticism, one that melds East and West into a whole new synthesis. To do this we must look to the future; that is our responsibility. We middle-management spirituality-teacher types are beginning to get a hint of the colossal task ahead. It may take seven hundred years, such is the resistance of materialism with its built-in incentives and rewards. Usually when I tell people this they reply, "Okay, guess I'll go back to worrying about myself and ignoring that long-term nonsense." Unless you have a mind that practically thinks in terms of geological epochs, my mission statement probably will not make sense to you. There is no reason why it should—except that those of us who think in terms of geological epochs would like you to try to understand.

Exercise 12: You Are the Mystic

Let's return to one of the practices I described above: imagining yourself as you would be if you were deep into the work of the mystic.

See if you can actually think of yourself as the mystic who sits before you in your mind's eye. It will seem to you that such a person has certain powers of manipulation that you presently do not. What would you do with these powers if you had them? Where would your responsibilities lie?

Let's try another tack: What would the mystic be thinking? What would he or she be contemplating? How do such persons regard their fellow beings? This quote from Pir Vilayat provides a clue: "When we judge others, we are certainly judging the Artist who has created them. If we realized this, it would not be difficult to feel the presence of God everywhere."

Meditate on this phrase. See how it applies to your personality and your life. Try it on as an ideal. In this way you will slowly begin to create the being that you imagine you can be. You have begun to cocreate with God.

When people are initiated into the Sufi Order, they are told never to assign themselves a practice. Why? Because we are the worst judges of our own state. You will not see the forest of yourself for the trees. For the longest time, you will not even see the tree of yourself for the branch of yourself. You will need an outside observer. Do not be offended; this is true of everybody. It was not unusual for the Pir to ask people he trusted to be honest with him about what he was doing himself or how he was teaching—or even how he looked. And, of course, he had his own spiritual guide.

If the Pir could submit to this discipline, so can you.

God-Realization

I would like to conclude this chapter with a few words about attaining God-realization. Needless to say, I approach this subject with extreme caution. I am hesitant to presume to say very much about it at all. I do not want to create the impression that God-realization is something that can even be talked about. It is not, not any more than the color blue is something you can talk about with someone who has been blind from birth.

Nevertheless, despite my disclaimers, I will say this:

God-realization is God realizing you, not you realizing God. Few go to this extreme of God-realization—of allowing God to realize them. Why? I suppose because finally it is extremely difficult, almost impossible, for us to break our attachment to separation.

People who do not attain God-realization are no less valid than those who do. It is simply that there is an area of creative reality in which the former will not participate. Those who will one day attain God-realization are driven by a sort of inborn compulsion; that is all. Whatever you do is fine. What you do is what you need to do. The important thing is your presence, your openness, to God.

What is the role of your spiritual guide in this? With regard to God-realization, he or she expresses the Beloved's experience of *Nasut*—physical reality—and seeks to look upon you with the love of all Creation. Sometimes you will see that look of love in the eyes of your guide. For some, it is enough to bask in that warmth; for a very few others, the need to see what the guide sees is a mighty force pushing them to the edge of what it is possible for humans to experience. If you come to that edge, you become what Pir Vilayat calls the Cocreator. Then, God looks directly through your eyes and acts purposefully on the earth plane. There is no pretending about this state. It is the real thing.

So, as I so often advise, watch your breath, do your meditations, and wait and see what comes.

Your fate is in your own hands.

The spiritual knowledge is never taught.
Even the initiator cannot teach it in words; it is imparted,
and that comes without words.
—Hazrat Inayat Khan

10

THE RETREAT

It was late 1998. I was headed down the highway in my fifteen-year-old Plymouth Voyager van on my way to an individual two-week spiritual retreat where I would entrust my soul to a guide I did not know very well.

And I got lost.

I never get lost. I always know where north is, and east and south and west. They had me teach map orientation in the Army because of this skill. But now, on my way to this retreat, driving fifty miles per hour instead of my usual sixty-plus, asking myself twice as often as usual, "Am I doing the right thing?"— I got lost.

I stopped the van, looked at the map, figured out where I was, and continued on my way.

Was getting lost a sign or an omen of some kind? It could have been, or maybe it was an indication of the anxiety I was feeling. I had had a lot of retreat experience at this point, but I knew this one would somehow be different. Knowingly approaching the unknown can have that effect.

At 3:30 that afternoon I pulled up in front of the modest ranch house where I was to spend the next two weeks. No one was home. My guide had told me she would not be back until four. Actually, I had deliberately arrived early in order to reconnoiter the place by myself. The feel of a place you go to on a retreat is important; it has to be a psychic space that is appropriate to your soul. I decided the feel of this place was fine. The front yard was neat, but not fussily so. The neighborhood was unusually quiet—or so it seemed to me, and so I hoped, and as it turned out, so it was. I walked around to the back of the house where the retreat hut was supposed to be. There it was, an eight-by-ten-foot building painted white and tucked into a corner of the yard. I opened the door and went into this one-room cubicle I was to occupy for two weeks. It had a cot neatly made up with an unpretentious quilt, an electric heater, a small table that obviously served as a kind of altar, and an electric tea kettle. That was it. The walls had recently been painted white, but there were no decorations. I would come to appreciate this lack of decoration; no decoration equals no visual distraction. I approved of my new quarters and went back to the van to get my bags.

Once I had carried my things into the hut, I took out my camera. I am an amateur photographer. I like taking photos, and I wanted to give my personality something to do. The personality acts up at the beginning of a retreat; it does not want to be doing this in the first place, it feels challenged, even threatened—as well it should, since the personality hates change, and I had come on this retreat to see about some changes. At times like this you have to trick the personality into cooperating. You have to soothe it and distract it, and so I was letting it take pictures.

I stopped taking photos when my guide arrived. I will not describe her personally because, for purposes of this retreat, she did not have a personality; she was my guide. She invited me into the main house for tea and conversation, but it soon became obvious even to me that my conversational ability was rapidly disappearing in the light of the forthcoming experience. It was not long before she showed me where things were, explained the routine to me, and deftly deposited me back at the retreat hut.

I approved of her style as much as I approved of the hut, and I knew that this was going to be a good retreat. It had to be. I was hoping to transform myself. Not that I had expectations. You have to try to have no expectations when you go on a retreat; otherwise, your expectations will interfere with what can happen. But to transform myself was my subliminal intent.

I had made extraordinary preparations for this retreat. I had quit smoking two months before, in part so that I would not have the baggage of cigarettes to drag into the retreat. I had quit reading fiction in anticipation of this retreat, and I had started rising at 3:00 a.m. to meditate (a recommended practice in spiritual circles anyway). I had brought nothing to read, and I had vowed to write nothing. I would not listen to music even though I knew it would be offered, music being a popular adjunct to meditation. I was going to stick to the normal retreat diet, though I knew that if I insisted I could get more varied fare: there would be no coffee; no animal products, including dairy and eggs; no spices. I had a supply of aspirin for coffee withdrawal symptoms. There would be no talking at all. All communication, at least on my part, would be by written note only; my no-writing vow would not be broken if the notes were restricted to essential communications such as "I'm out of granola" and the like. The no-talking vow included avoiding as much as possible contact with anyone but my guide. Even contact with my guide would be restricted to our having a short daily meditation together, usually in the evening just before dinner. In the days to come, I would learn to appreciate the respect my guide and her husband paid to these vows of mine. Whenever I entered their house—to use the bathroom was the usual reason; sometimes I would be replenishing my eating supplies—they would disappear behind closed doors. They were sensitive to my whereabouts and always made sure to avoid me in my rare comings and goings, and I really valued that.

An important part of the retreat process is how much personal baggage you leave behind, and I had never left so much behind before. This was the first time I had given up cigarettes. At previous retreats, I had always taken a book to read—a respected Sufi text, of course!—and part of my idea of who I am is that I am a reader. At previous retreats, I had always taken copious notes. I had usually finagled a way to have coffee in the morning. But all that had meant that, although I was doing the prescribed practices, I was not really doing the retreat. This time, I was really doing the retreat.

So there I was, fully prepared, with vow in hand, support system set aside, ready to begin. And that is what I did: I began. Nothing dramatic, nothing difficult. I was given a list of practices and I started doing them. As regimens go, I suppose it was not bad. It went like this:

- Rise at 6:00 a.m.
- Go outside and wait for sunrise. While waiting for sunrise, do pre-sunrise meditations.
- Do fairly simple meditation and purification practices until 8:00 a.m.
- Have breakfast. Take a shower. Get back to work.
- Meditation and other practices until noon.
- Two-hour break. A nap and maybe a walk.
- More practices, until 6:00 p.m., at which point the guide comes and gives the regimen for the following day.

- Dinner.
- Movie—I'm kidding about the movie. But I did get a hot meal.
- More meditation, until 10:00 p.m.
- Lights out.
- Up at 3:00 a.m. for meditation.
- Go back to sleep.
- Start the whole thing over again at 6:00 a.m.

Does this sound easy? Bear in mind that, except for my brief and infrequent contacts with my guide, I was alone in a one-room hut (or just outside it, sitting in an armchair) for twenty-four hours a day. Furthermore, I had made an agreement not just to be alone but not to seek anyone out, not even an all-night grocery store clerk. I had a great many odd things to do, like repeating words for an hour at a time in a foreign language, usually Arabic or Sanskrit, occasionally ancient Greek or Hebrew. Sound easy? Try repeating the following for an hour (I will let you off easy and give you some English words):

"Toward the one, united with all." Go ahead, try it. I'll wait. The personality hates all this. I did discover (as I had discovered on earlier shorter retreats) that if I allowed the personality to kvetch while I more or less ignored it, then it was happy and I could get on with my work. After a few days on a retreat, the personality gets bored with itself and stops—or slows down, anyway. It still pops up from time to time with a remembered slight or some other complaint, but mostly it stays quiet. In my case, eventually—after eight or nine days—it actually began to enjoy the discipline.

For the neophyte as well as the experienced meditator, all of this is a struggle. Everything worthwhile always is. You just must not let it bother you.

Eventually the retreat ended.

I had the obligatory post-retreat assessment session with my guide. Then I got into my antiquated Plymouth Voyager van and drove back home—only this time I was driving my usual sixty miles per hour and not fifty. I was not half as worried as I had been when I was coming, and I did not get lost. Then I was back in my old life—but with a difference. I had just done, and you will have just done if you do it, something that very few of my or your acquaintances will ever understand or even know about. Witness this conversation:

"Hey, Phillip, how was your vacation?"

"Wonderful! I went on a retreat."

"Really—! What's that?"

You will get to the point—I am at that point now—where you simply tell your friends and acquaintances where you went, but you do not tell them what you did there. I have to say, though, that I am getting much freer now about revealing what I do. So are other Sufi friends of mine. We are getting the impression that the Western world has finally reached the point where it likes to know that some of its members are seriously pursuing an inner life. The people who like to know are not planning to emulate such pursuits, but they admire them in the same way they admire a priest or a rabbi who prays for their soul.

Perhaps you are thinking that I have left something out. Are you wondering what happened to me during my retreat? Are you wondering if I was transformed?

It is not quite true to say that when I went on this retreat I was looking to be entirely transformed. I was not looking for anything. As I have already mentioned, when you go on a retreat you should have no expectations at all. Expectations get in the way. The most effective way to do a retreat is to decide at the beginning to do the work and just let whatever comes, come.

The retreat can have a goal, or a theme, like healing or entering into a sacred space—but even here you are merely providing a focus, not positing a result. The instant you prejudge result, you have lost that result.

Moreover, you are not as much in charge of matters as you might think. The Koran says: "God raises up who He will." That is why, for the purists, doing the retreat is reason enough in itself; it is its own reward (I am not sure I subscribe to this view, but it might help you to keep it in mind). So, no, I definitely did not go into this retreat expecting to come out of it a clone of Saint Francis of Assisi (though I am only human; the thought might have crossed my mind—you can never be completely sure about these things—but chances were highly unlikely). Nevertheless, something did happen to me—though I am not particularly anxious to tell you about it, for two reasons: (1) nothing I have ever experienced is any different from the experiences of thousands of other mystics who have written about such experiences far more eloquently than I ever will; and (2) the only way to understand what I am talking about is to do it. This is a book of encouragement, not a book of description. So, be encouraged. But perhaps I will lift the veil a little for you.

Imagine yourself sitting in a small one-room retreat hut following a disciplined routine such as I have described above, and arriving at a place where your personality finally gives up protesting and agrees to go along with you in this bizarrely ab errational experience you are having.

What do you feel?

You feel very calm.

It might have taken you eight or nine days to get to this state—not eight or nine days of increasing wonder and awe as the blessed state comes ever closer, but eight or nine days of "Why in the world did I ever agree to do this?" (occasionally punctuated by the exclamation, "Oh, that's why!"). I can only speak for myself—perhaps your own experience will be different—but I will tell you that there can come a point in the retreat when total relaxation seems to be the most natural state in the world. This is relaxation at a level most people never experience, because they are never able to escape from their worldly cares long enough to be able to. Body, mind, emotion, and soul are in harmony; all of them are comfortable and glowing. It is at moments like this that you begin to suspect there may be something behind notions like the "One Being." Maybe it is all true, you say to yourself; maybe I really am a part of a greater whole, a greater whole that I in turn encompass.

I would like to list some points you should keep in mind to help you attain some success in any retreat you might take. (Bear in mind that my retreat of fifteen days, all alone, was a medium-size retreat, the longest being forty days. The student of Sufism usually begins the retreat experience with a three-day retreat—though I often have a first-timer do just two days. After a few two- or three-day retreats, the neophyte advances to a six-day retreat, six days being the length of the basic annual maintenance retreat. I think this is where most people stop, if for no other reasons than practical ones. In modern-day society, it is difficult to devote more than a week solely to yourself. Every time I go off to do a retreat, there is a part of me that feels a little guilty about abandoning Majida for a week (not that she has ever given me any reason for thinking I should feel guilty). But here are the points:

- Attitude is all-important. Your attitude determines what sort of retreat you have. If you want your retreat to be transformative, your attitude has to be one of total submission. I am not saying you should be wimpily involved in a masochistic relationship with God. You do not even have to give up your opinions—though a strong suspicion of their validity would be helpful. I am saying that total submission means allowing the power of the practices and meditations to work on you while, at the same time, you firmly separate yourself from your day-to-day support systems.

- Along with right attitude, you must allow yourself to retain the capacity for being surprised. There is a kind of innocent honesty—a sort of naïveté, I suppose—that carries us forward when opinion and knowledge hold us back. When Majida and I do our retreats, we try simply to do the assigned practices without thinking much about anything else. Thinking about the other things is the job of the retreat guide.
- At the end of all this—I allude to it often in this book—is God-realization.

This is not something that a person strives to attain or even seeks. Try to remember that God-realization is not about your realizing God; it is about God realizing you. To put it another way: you try to get good enough at the meditations that you realize the capacity to step aside and allow a direct experience of God's realization of Him- or Herself to occur through you. Since this requires that you no longer be present as a discrete volitional entity, most people are uncomfortable even with the idea, let alone the reality. And, admittedly, it does require a certain calm assurance on your part that you will get your mind and body back! It can take a great deal of work to arrive at this place. On the other hand, sometimes it just happens. The great Sufi metaphysician Ibn 'Arabi is said to have attained God-realization within three days of his first retreat, when he was eighteen years old. Which might cause you to say to yourself, "Well, goody for him!" We each have our path, and we each have our personal expression of the divine. Comparisons only cause distress or, occasionally, arrogance. So learn to relax, discover repose, and let's see what happens.

Here and there throughout this book, I talk about Muhasaba, the continual examination of conscience. The constant practice of Muhasaba will help you know, at every point, who you think you are, and such knowledge will help you at every point on the spiritual path, not the least when you embark upon the retreat.

The image of who we are becoming is our guide. The retreat is simply part of that process of becoming.

The seeking for God is a natural outcome of the maturity of the soul. There is a time in life when a passion is awakened in the soul which gives the soul a longing for the unattainable, and if the soul does not take that direction, then it certainly misses something in life which is its innate longing and in which lies its ultimate satisfaction.

—Hazrat Inayat Khan

11

A Passion
for the
Unattainable

Ever since I can remember, I have felt the dull throb of an emotional need that it seemed could never be satisfied.

Nothing could ease the throb. I tried sex—I suppose everyone does—which only worked for a short time; drugs, which masked the need but did not fill it; coffee and cigarettes, cigarettes especially, which dulled the need and covered it over with a smokescreen. I tried science-fiction novels, which enabled me to ignore the throb for the length of time it took to read the novel. Whatever I tried—without any conscious idea, really, of what I was trying to do—failed to fill the aching void that seemed to be in me every waking and possibly every sleeping moment.

It was not until I quit smoking that I began to come to grips with this throb. This was because when I quit smoking, I felt it with renewed vigor and realized that that was what I had been trying to cover up with the smoking. At first, I thought this redoubled throb was due to nicotine deprivation. But when long after the symptoms of nicotine deprivation should have gone away I still felt the throb in all its power, I realized it was something that had to do with the human soul—and I started to wonder how many other people were experiencing this same background emotional noise. I wondered if the whole human race might not be feeling it. And I came to the conclusion that the throb was simply that spiritual yearning of which all the ecstatic poets speak. What is the best way I have personally found for dealing with this primal longing? It is twofold: through meditation and through the expression of my creativity, which for me involves crafting beautiful objects in my workshop.

Hazrat Inayat Khan writes, "When the light of love has been lit, the heart becomes transparent, so that the intelligence of the soul can see through it; but until the heart is kindled by the flame of love, the intelligence, which is constantly yearning to experience life on the surface, is groping in the dark."

THE LIMITATIONS OF POSSESSIONS

There are many different ways of trying to assuage the passion for the unattainable. Not all are satisfactory. One popular means is by acquiring possessions. But acquiring possessions (and those possessions can be friends as well as things) is only another of those gropings in the dark that Hazrat Inayat Khan mentions in the quotation above. It is a groping that makes us feel alive, but only temporarily. Possessions do satisfy our longings—but only for a moment. Hazrat Inayat Khan does not say anywhere that giving up possessions helps kindle our heart into a flame of love. The path of the renunciation of worldly goods is encouraged by some, but it is not the Sufi way. Sufism holds that we should awaken within life, not outside it. It declares that our hearts can be on fire with love even if we own a nice car, even a Rolls-Royce. The important thing to understand is that the Rolls-Royce, although it is a nice car, is just a car and will not satisfy our yearning to experience our being at its fullest. Having stuff brings only fleeting satisfaction. It also brings permanent problems, because if you have stuff you have to pay attention to that stuff. Every day that I go into my cabinetmaker's shop I look around and take a mental inventory of my tools, right down to the drill bits, and I have hundreds of those. This clutters up my mind. My mind is further cluttered up by the resentment and disapproval that well up within me each time I take this inventory; I think of the tools I do not have, of the perfect stranger who messed up one I do have, and so on and so forth. When you consider that my shop-inventory resentments are then shoved into the usual pile of resentments we all have— he done me wrong, she done me wrong, it done me wrong, and so on, and so on—you can imagine how totally cluttered up my mind really is.

(Our minds are, in fact, so continually and constantly cluttered up that we have to wonder just how far we can even know what we are thinking or feeling in any one regard. The Sufis have a number of techniques for knowing this. Muhasaba is one of them—the practice of self-criticism and self-interrogation. Muhasaba is fairly easy. Ask yourself, "What am I doing right now?" When the answer comes, whatever it may be, ask the question again, then again. Try to avoid rationalizing. Practice Muhasaba every day. Always question what you are doing. This is not to say that everything you are doing is wrong! No, of course not. But you need to be totally aware of how you are going about your day and totally aware of your thoughts about how you are going about your day. This is Muhasaba. It is akin to the mindfulness of the Buddhists.)

THE COFFEE SHOP THAT REFUSED TO BE SEPARATE

Sex, smoking, food, drink, having possessions—these are not the only ways we have of temporarily appeasing our yearning for the unattainable. There are a hundred other ways. Let me give you an example. This example is a sequel to the two-week retreat I discussed at great length in the last chapter. You will remember that I spent those two weeks—actually, fifteen days—isolated from the world in a small hut. Because the main constituents of my diet were granola, apple juice, and rice cakes, by the time the retreat was over, I was experiencing a high degree of grease deprivation. I had not had a New York coffee-shop breakfast of meat, eggs, toast, and hash browns for that whole two weeks.

As I was getting into my car, I asked my retreat guide where the nearest restaurant was that I could get a good New York-style breakfast. She was at something of a loss, perhaps reluctant to tell me because she was a vegetarian herself. But she finally came through with the name of a place, and I left at top speed, stopping on the way only to buy a *New York Times*. (I was also suffering from a high degree of *New York Times* crossword puzzle deprivation.) I arrived at the designated restaurant, plunked myself down at the counter, and in one breath placed my order:

"Two poached on wheat toast, bacon, hash browns, coffee." The man behind the counter stared at me. I remembered I was not in a New York City coffee shop and repeated my order slowly. Soon my breakfast arrived (a compromise: fried eggs, no hash browns, this not being New York), and I set to.

I was halfway through my breakfast and not quite halfway through my crossword puzzle (this was Friday, and the puzzles are harder on Friday) when a voice came over the public address system: "Ladies and gentlemen, it is now time to say the Pledge of Allegiance to the Flag of the United States of America. Will everyone please rise and face the flag?"

My first thought was that my retreat guide had made a mistake and directed me into a parallel universe, one where the U.S. government was a touch more dictatorial. I looked around and saw that if this were a parallel universe, it was an extremely good copy of my own. Furthermore, everybody was standing up. I looked at the guy sitting next to me, who seemed as confused as I was. But we shrugged at one another and did what any sane person would do when confronted with the customs of a foreign country: we stood up, said the Pledge of Allegiance along with everyone else, and sat down again to finish our breakfasts. (My crossword puzzle had to wait; it was too hard—I finished it on a coffee break farther along on my way home.)

The owner of the coffee shop had found a way to assuage his feelings of separation, his desire for the unattainable. It was by making everyone join him for a brief moment of union in the recitation of the Pledge of Allegiance. It was not much of a union, really; it was just a gesture in that direction. But I could feel the satisfaction that even the regular customers must have felt—for they had fallen into the moment readily to assuage their own feelings of separation—at performing this well-known and at the same time slightly unusual ritual.

(The regulars may even have felt a bit of smug defiance toward those strangers, like myself, who had essentially been forced to conform to the ritual. That was okay with me. We all have these moments of smug defiance, and I was not offended. If anything, I was charmed. This is not to say that I intend to make the Pledge of Allegiance a part of my daily meditation regime. But I instantly had a sense of the deeper resonances of my encounter with patriotism in that small-town coffee shop.)

No matter how veiled from us the secrets of the greater cosmos seem to be, we all still feel the need to express our commitment to that greater cosmos. We cannot shake the belief that there must be some way of acknowledging our innate belongingness to a whole greater than our world. My friends in the small-town coffee shop had found one way of acknowledging that belongingness.

The Unendingness of the Passion for the Unattainable

Our passion for the unattainable, that aching desire we have to experience ourselves as being a part of something greater than ourselves, finds expression in the world all around us. I have said that meditation and the exercise of meaningful creativity (in my case woodworking) can bring us closer to satisfying this yearning. A number of professional healers, all of them working out there in the real world, come to the Sufi Center that Majida and I direct. There is a chiropractor; there are a couple of physical therapists; there is a polarity therapist; there is a nurse practitioner. There are a number of accomplished healers who, technically speaking, are not professionals. When I hear these people talking about healing, often I hear them expressing the intense creative joy they sometimes experience as they do their healing. They talk about practicing healing just like I talk about making furniture. All of us know we are impacting our environment in a meaningful way. All of us know it, and that knowledge makes us high.

I have already quoted Hazrat Inayat Khan:

The seeking for God is a natural outcome of the maturity of the soul. There is a time in life when a passion is awakened in the soul which gives the soul a longing for the unattainable, and if the soul does not take that direction, then it certainly misses something in life which is its innate longing and in which lies its ultimate satisfaction. . . . We are born with the thinking of the whole universe, but as our consciousness becomes limited to what we think we are as an individual, we lose the thinking of the universe and base our knowledge upon our experience, or upon our way of interpreting experience. When we rediscover that thinking, we realize how inadequate our personal thinking is.

There is no end to the yearning for the unattainable, not even for the best of us. Once I was driving the Pir to Kennedy Airport when he suddenly said to me, "I'm seventy-five years old and only now am I understanding what it means to be a Sufi." I was not quite sure how to respond to this unexpected announcement, so I said nothing. The Pir's admission told me a lot about spiritual progress. My own breakthroughs come at ten-year intervals—or so it seems, maybe because each one of them is so exhausting that it takes me nine years to work up the courage to try for another breakthrough. Or maybe it just seems that way; maybe the intervals are a whole lot shorter. The fact is that we need only look at how attached we all are to, well, just about everything, to understand why the intervals must indeed be so very long.

Exercise 13: Being Greater

This practice demands that we be continuously aware of the limitation of our experience and the probability that there is other, as yet undiscovered, territory waiting to open itself before us. For the next minute or so, try to imagine that what you know is bigger than you know. If you honestly try this, you will experience a sort of psychic stretching. Do you remember when you were a kid and you tried to blow up a new balloon, and right at the start it seemed like it would be impossible to blow it up? When you feel a psychic stretching and feel like you cannot stretch any more, think of that balloon—and then relax into the exercise and allow the soul's desire to take shape. How do you do this? You can facilitate this allowing by calmly remembering that who the world says you are is only a tiny portion of your being. Remember, too, that "up" and "out" and all those other words are merely words. Everything that is, is there within you.

Sometimes, when I am explaining the above, a student will exclaim, "I never imagined God was unattainable!" I am not saying God is unattainable. The unattainable, when we are talking about the passion for the unattainable, simply refers to that state in which you have an intimation of the actual vastness of creation. This is not an intellectual or a philosophical experience but a direct perception of reality, one known about and sought after by every mystical order. What I have been trying to do is point to the existence of this experience without actually being able to describe it, because, as in so many things in the world of the mystics, words are useless in this respect and all we can really do is talk around the subject.

As I have said before, Westerners have a peculiar attitude toward spirituality. We expect to get something back when we put something in; we want value for value; we expect a return on our investment. I am not being critical. That is simply how we are.

No one from the East thinks that just because he or she is expending effort something ought to happen. Easterners are more likely to trust the word of the teacher that expending effort is sufficient unto itself. For the man or woman of the East, a passion for the unobtainable is a perfectly normal thing. (You can even turn the notion on its head and say, as in the East, that a passion for the unattainable is God's testing of God's own limits, this being a dynamic our psyche must translate into its own personal terms if we are to understand it at all.)

Hazrat Inayat Khan writes:

There are different grades of exaltation.

To the Sufi, the soul is a current that joins the physical body to the source. And the art of repose naturally makes it easier for the soul to experience freedom, inspiration, power, because it is then loosened from the grip of the physical body. As Rumi says in the *Masnavi*, "Man is a captive on earth. His body and his mind are his prison bars. And the soul is unconsciously craving to experience once again the freedom which originally belonged to it." The Platonic idea about reaching the higher source is the same: that by exaltation the soul, so to speak, rises above the fast hold of the physical body; it may be only for a few moments, but it experiences in those moments a freedom which man has never experienced before.

A moment of exaltation is a different experience at every level. The supreme exaltation is hinted at in the Bible: "Be ye perfect even as your Father in heaven is perfect." Many religious people will say that it is impossible for man to be perfect; but it is said in the Bible just the same. At all times the knowers and seers have understood that there is a stage at which, by touching a particular phase of existence, one feels raised above the limitations of life, and is given that power and peace and freedom, that light and life, which belong to the source of all beings. In other words, in that moment of supreme exaltation one is not only united with the source of all beings, but dissolved in it; for the source is one's self.

This is heady territory; we are talking about the unattainable. When I first started looking into the spiritual life, I thought the sorts of experiences described above were just around the corner, and all I had to do to have them was express a desire, meditate for twenty minutes or so, and bingo, there I was. Now I know better. But I am not saying that the experiences described above are beyond our grasp. They are absolutely not. Note that Hazrat Inayat Khan quotes from the Bible (he did this in many of his lectures): "Be ye perfect even as your Father in Heaven is perfect." Murshid used this quotation in many contexts, but his meaning was always the same: perfection is attainable, and its attainment should be our objective. We have the capability of revisiting that state to which Rumi refers when he says in the *Masnavi*, "The soul is unconsciously craving to experience once again the freedom which originally belonged to it."

THE UNVEILING OF NEW UNIVERSES

Think about it. For some reason that you cannot remember, you, or whatever it is that presently identifies itself as you, deliberately decided to give up freedom in order to put on the fetters of physical existence. Why in the world would anyone want to do this? The classic answer is that in experiencing freedom within limitations, we break the bonds of conventional creation and force new universes to unveil themselves. We demand that our beings allow what is unknown but possible to express itself within us, even though that seems impossible. What comes

154

may, to our limited minds, look like a totally altered reality, even though it was really already there. The difficulty in achieving this is that we tend to concentrate on our limitations, believing they are us. But we are not our limitations; what we are is that aspect of the divine that is resolving the paradox, or, as Pir Vilayat constantly put it, "reconciling the irreconcilables."

But once we have been born on earth, a fascinating thing begins to happen. Despite our feelings of desperation and separation, we genuinely begin to feel this passion for the unattainable; and, recognizing that above all else we are driven to fulfill it, we submit ourselves to a spiritual discipline and begin to realize that our limitations are not us. This is exciting—or it can be, and it should be—because it is the very knowledge of our personal limitations and our broader human and physical reality-based limitations that allows us to ignore these limitations and step outside them, if only for a nanosecond. Thus are we able to turn reality on its head and experience God experiencing creation.

Once you have done this, nothing is ever the same again.

You have discovered you are not alone.

"A passion for the unattainable" is only a metaphysical way of saying that all the universes, all the various planes of existence, are finally a very big place. The beauty of it is that we human beings have the capacity to grasp a great deal of that very big place. We cannot have it all; there is too much, and some areas are restricted to particular beings (just trust me on this one). But we can have a lot.

What is equally interesting is that no two people carry exactly the same items into the universes. We each bring a little something unique to ourselves. Within the spiral model of creation—by which I mean that human evolution has the quality of appearing circular, of appearing repetitive, but it is really

155

always advancing upward—each person contributes something, and the complex interplay of all our contributions creates an amazingly balanced energy form, or it can. This actually works only when everyone links up. At the animalistic level, we call this energy a mob. At the angelic level, we call it the music of the spheres.

I guess most of us are stuck somewhere in between, sounding our plaintive individual notes and hoping someone will harmonize with us. Hang out with the Sufis long enough, and you will eventually hear them say in some way or another that not only do they want you to sing well, but they want you to sing right out to the limit of your capabilities—which are always going to be bigger than you think they are, plus a little.

The heart that is free of love sickness isn't a heart at all. The body deprived of the pangs of love is nothing but clay and water.

—Jami

12

LOVE

There are three kinds of love. The first is love in the marketplace. Here we bargain with our partner. We say, "Love me, and I might reciprocate," or, "I love you, and I demand that you reciprocate." The second is the love that sees others as beings to be tolerated, with quirks we perhaps accept. This is better than the first kind of love. The third is that love wherein you see all others as part and parcel of Allah. This is the best kind of love. It cannot be faked.

It is the Sufi kind of love.

THE VALUE OF VULNERABILITY

At the personal level, trust is an essential component of love. You have to give your trust to someone in such a way that you are vulnerable to that person's every whim—maybe not totally vulnerable, but certainly very vulnerable. Let's talk about vulnerability.

Pir-o-Murshid writes: "He who guards himself against being fooled by another is clever; he who does not allow another to fool him is wise; he who is fooled by another is a simpleton;

159

but he who knowingly allows himself to be fooled shows the character of the saint."

An old friend of mine once did her best to convince me that we have to be in a state of total vulnerability when we encounter someone else. She felt that only then did we have a chance of penetrating through to the real nature of that person. Of course, she understood that you courted being rebuffed when you acted in this way. But she felt the risk was worth taking, that being rebuffed would be a welcome price to pay in light of the highly rewarding results that could come your way if you maintained this state of vulnerability. Such was my friend's assertion, and I was not happy with what she had said. But, as we went on talking, I realized that what I was not happy about was the possibility of humiliation. Imagine going up to someone with whom you are fairly certain you have nothing in common—someone you are sure you do not like and who you are sure either does not like you or out of some lofty sense of superiority would rather just ignore you—imagine going up to that person and saying, "Let's talk!" Probably when you picture yourself doing this—and imagine what the results might be—you find yourself saying, "Love may be universal, but I think I'll let somebody else work with this guy." At least, such was my initial reaction to what my friend was saying.

But, as the discussion continued, I realized that what she was proposing was what I do anyway. I have not approached people from whom I am totally alienated, but I have approached people in a spirit of curiosity, or maybe just because I had never gotten to know them and felt I should. I once approached someone who flat-out told me she could not think of a single reason why we should talk. That was very embarrassing—but I got over it. I think my friend who advocates total vulnerability is right: vulnerability is the key to trust. And trust is the key to love.

I am not saying you should deliberately seek out someone you do not like and make a huge effort to understand that person—or maybe I *am* saying that. But I am not passionately encouraging such action. What I am saying is that often the greatest barrier to feeling comfortable with another person, or the greatest barrier to any kind of interpersonal communication, is the unwillingness to be vulnerable.

Being vulnerable is the key to spirituality. You do not progress just by knowing. You progress by surrendering all or at least a portion of your knowledge. In so doing, you create a sort of vacuum, a vulnerability that God can crown by filling you with a divinely inspired curiosity and awareness. Maybe God sees it like this: by being vulnerable, on a personal level you have created an accommodation in yourself, enabling someone else to participate in your experience. Such accommodations open us out to higher levels of accommodation.

Do unto others, and eventually God does unto you.

Meditation is a state of emotional and spiritual vulnerability. In meditating, you open yourself to whatever (or whomever— the Beloved?) comes along. You accommodate yourself to the possibility of responding to God's intentions on this world's stage. (Just do not assume that that is what you are doing!) Meditation has many purposes, but the one I am talking about here is that of creating a vulnerability to the spirit of the Be- loved—and, on this personal level, the approach of the Beloved is really about your own soul's coming closer. I have not heard it for a while, but is that old soul-mate business still making the rounds? When I hear that phrase I always think, "What, only one?" As if in this whole wide universe there were only one soul that resonates perfectly with yours! I believe it is not the idea of having a soul mate, but the idea of being rescued, that appeals to us. Rescued from what? For one thing, from the annoying need to be vulnerable and therefore risk the even more annoying experience of being humiliated.

Love is not about finding a soul mate. If it seems to be at the beginning, the feeling starts to dissipate the moment you and your soul mate discover how different your toothpaste habits are. Rather, love is about exploring vulnerability, about exploring degrees of acceptance of and resistance to each other. On the spiritual level, it is about continuously reaching for deeper and deeper levels of trust in God.

All this is scary. Here is an exercise that might help:

Exercise 14: Entering the Soul of Another

Choose a person you would like to understand better—a friend, your teacher if you are in a spiritual group, an acquaintance. Imagine that that person is before you. Imagine gradually entering into that other's body, getting inside that other's skin.

Enter into the thoughts of that person; imagine how he or she thinks.

Try to get behind the thoughts to the deeper motivations.

That is the first step. It is difficult, because the closer you are to a person, the harder it is to know what that person is really like; how you see him or her is wrapped up with how you see yourself and your relationship. For the purposes of this exercise, it might be helpful for you to pretend your knowledge of that person is incorrect or at least incomplete. There are a good many things you do not know, and your object in this exercise is to find out what some of these things are. Now try to imagine that that person is as fully realized as she or he can possibly be at that particular moment. The key here is not to think of the other person in relationship to yourself; do not think of him or her as how you personally want that person to be, but rather try to think of the other as he or she really is or could be in light of that person's potential. You have to desire with all your heart that the other person realize his or her completeness—and you must bear in mind all the while that this completeness may not include you (it may—it probably will!—but if it does not, well, that's okay too).

It helps to see the person as surrounded by white light, as totally pure, totally without guile, completely innocent, yet spiritually mature.

This practice is intended to give you an insight you might not otherwise have had into the other person. It is also meant to create an accommodation for transformation for both of you. You are dedicating a portion of your psychic support to that person. He or she is free to accept or reject that support, but it can only be rejected if it is offered.

Vulnerability can be periodic; think of being totally vulnerable as an ideal state, not one you have to be in every moment. Our psyches are delicate; regard vulnerability as a flower that opens up, then closes to collect itself for a time.

Hazrat Inayat Khan writes, "Enter unhesitatingly, Beloved, for in this abode there is naught but my longing for Thee. Do I call Thee my soul? But Thou art my spirit. Can I call Thee my life? But Thou livest forever. May I call Thee my Beloved? But Thou art Love itself. Then what must I call Thee? I must call Thee myself."

Our natural state, that from which we spring, is pure and innocent, and knows itself as an essence, maybe *the* essence, of divine love. Then we are born, and we forget. That does not mean love has deserted us. It is still there; we have just forgotten it. The call from within is a reminder: "Hey, remember me?" This love seems alien because it is so different from what we have grown to accept. But what is actually alien are the mistaken assumptions about love that our being in physical reality has engendered in us.

Once we have realized at least a part of this truth, the responsibility for all of us becomes one of further expanding the accommodation for divine love within our earthly beings, and of becoming a part of that effort toward greater evolution within the confines of limited existence in which all of humanity is involved.

In other words, we are really all in this together, in ways most of us never realize. But the Sufis have realized that for a very long time, as we will now discuss.

LOVE AS *WADOOD*: THE FEELING THAT CREATED THE UNIVERSE

The word the Sufis use for love is the attribute of God called *Wadood*. It was out of this love that God created the universe.

Pir Vilayat writes: "From the solitude of its Unity, the Divine Being fragmented itself out of love for the possibility of you and me."

Imagine the quality of the energy that expresses itself by creating the immense vastnesses of the many planes of existence solely for the love of the possibility of you and me! Does that thought not make you feel a little better about your life?

Since Wadood is one of the divine qualities of God—one of what the Sufis call *Sifat*—we can make this quality of creation-engendering divine love manifest in ourselves by remembering and repeating the word *Wadood*. In so doing, we are concentrating on the divine archetype of Wadood/Love—Wadood as manifested in God—in such a way as to bring this quality down to earth, to incarnate it within our individual beings. This is difficult, to say the least. We will have to repeat the word *Wadood* with a mastery of every subtlety of the unique vibrational qualities possessed by its two syllables. But though this is difficult, it is possible.

LOVE AS *ISHQ*: DIVINE NOSTALGIA

Though *Wadood* is the word the Sufis commonly use for love, the word that Pir-o-Murshid was fonder of using in this sense was *Ishq*. Ishq expresses a divine love that is a kind of divine nostalgia—a longing that we all experience at a very deep level, even though we do not know exactly what the object of that longing is. This Ishq is a longing for a reunion with the Beloved, even if we are not certain who the Beloved is; it is an elusive sense of incompleteness that can be remedied only by communion with an undefined aspect of ourselves that is somehow very difficult to connect with, or even to understand. Such is the meaning of Ishq—at least as I currently understand it.

Hazrat Inayat Khan writes: "Is love pleasure, is love merriment? No, love is longing constantly; love is persevering unweariedly; love is hoping patiently; love is willing surrender; love is regarding constantly the pleasure and displeasure of the Beloved, for love is resignation to the will of the possessor of one's heart; it is love that teaches man: 'Thou, not I.'"

CHAPTER TWELVE

Just because I say Ishq is divine nostalgia—even just because Pir Vilayat says it!—does not mean you have to believe it. It may be that this description of love at a divine level strikes you as utterly maudlin and mawkish. "Are all Sufis lovesick adolescents?" you may well ask. And your question might not be completely inappropriate.

What we have to remember is that Pir Vilayat, and his father, and the long line of Sufi seers that came before them, speak from a very lofty level. Like eagles, they have soared into the sky. Like the highest-flying of all birds, they can settle on mountaintops that they then encourage us to reach. It is from this vantage point that they survey the cosmos and speak to us of the true nature of divine love.

You, and I, are not yet that eagle on the mountaintop. The seers speak from high above our own present level of attainment. Let us at least give them the benefit of the doubt. Perhaps, as you repeat *Wadood* and continue to reach for the divine impulse of love that gave birth to the created universe, you will begin to get a glimmering of what the ancients meant. Setting aside the lofty goal of reaching the mountaintop, you will, perhaps, at least be able to move beyond personal emotion to cosmic emotion. You cannot bring about this sort of shift in your soul if all you are thinking about is whether somebody loves you. Pir Vilayat constantly exhorted us to get into the thinking of the universe, to experience the greater manifestation of God experiencing existence. Love is a part of that, and once we begin truly to grasp this higher thinking of the universe, all those lesser manifestations of love will at one and the same time appear less important and more poignant.

Here is an exercise that is intended to help you soar to the mountaintop.

Exercise 15: The Flight of the Eagle

Put yourself in a state of relaxation, preferably with your spine straight. There should be enough tension in your muscles to keep you completely erect; the rest of you can be at rest. Imagine for a moment that all your knowledge of yourself has been suspended and that you are an innocent gazing at a blank slate. It will help you to try to imagine the state you were in when you were a small child. Try to remember what it was like to be totally involved in a new experience, completely engrossed by whatever happened to be in front of you (perhaps something that would seem silly to you as an adult).

Can you recall that state? Use any method you can to reproduce it. The idea is to withdraw from your personality for just a few moments and imagine that you possess an eagle's vision of the world—the vision of a lofty eagle, uninvolved in self. If you could actually become the eagle, how would your personality shift from its normal perspective? Look at the world from the mountaintop, or from the loftiness of the eagle's soaring flight. Try to detect what keeps you from seeing in this way. See if you can discover how you would have to change to soar or to alight on the mountaintop.

It has always fascinated me that the Sufi mystics use "love" as the reason behind existence.

Hazrat Inayat Khan writes, "My heart has become an ocean, Beloved, since Thou hast poured Thy love into it."

It has occurred to me to wonder whether this primordial expression of the idea of love as divine intent did not seep down into the consciousnesses of us all and still lies behind the various meanings of the word *love* that we have today. Is there, in every form of love that exists today—even the most banal—a touch of divine intention?

I can see God fragmenting Him/Herself, descending from the solitude of peace, out of love for the possibility of me and of you, of the stars and of the atoms.

—Pir Vilayat Inayat Khan, paraphrasing Ibn ʿArabi

13

THE LIGHT OF KNIGHTHOOD

In the 1830s, the power brokers of the Russian Empire decided that, in addition to consolidating their power around the Black Sea to protect the empire's only warm-water port, they needed to increase its tax base. Realizing that the Caucasus Mountains held innumerable villages that would fill that bill, they started to annex them—and ran right into a Naqshbandi Sufi sheikh by the name of Shamyl, who disagreed. With equal measures of religious fervor and political pragmatism, he cajoled, persuaded, and coerced his fellow hillmen, many of whom were also Sufi initiates, to fight.

In reading of this conflict, what I found interesting, besides the details of the struggle, was that Shamyl's sheikh, his teacher, was a total pacifist and would not carry weapons. In fact, there were two entirely separate types of Sufis in the Caucasus. Most were in the fighter mold that one would expect among proud, independent mountain tribesmen; but some, like Shamyl's sheikh, were dedicated pacifists. The two groups accepted and supported each other.

What happened in the war? Eventually, the Russians simply wore them down. They had more men. They had more matériel. They prevailed through sheer attrition and a willingness to accept appalling losses. But it took thirty years. One hundred and forty years later, the descendants of those same Naqshbandi Sufis took their country back from the disintegrating Soviet empire. This is the country now known as Chechnya.

I have told this story to show that pacifism is not necessarily a Sufi quality. We tend to think that warrior-priests should only fight battles of the ego. But it seems God sometimes has a different task in mind for the Sufi: direct physical combat, as in the case of Chechnya.

Was Shamyl right to wage war? In light of today's bloody conflict between Russia and Chechnya, we might think not. But I believe we are too far removed from events to judge. We are relatively safe in the United States today and unlikely to face what Shamyl faced. But his story demonstrates that, to a certain degree, the knight must be a knight in the world; Sufi mystics need to know as much as they can about every aspect of the human condition.

If we wish to explore this aspect of the Sufi light of knighthood—that is, the Sufi as warrior-knight in the world—we first have to examine the relationship between the two states of being that the Sufis call *Wahid* and *Ahad*: Multiplicity in Unity, and Unity in Multiplicity.

To explore properly the relationship between these two states, we first have to try to understand the state the Sufis call *Dhat*, or *Zat*, which underlies Wahid and Ahad. In seeking to understand these states of being, we are seeking to understand no less than the nature of God! It is good to be mindful of the words of the tenth-century Sufi master al-Hujwiri in the *Kashf*

172

al-Mahjub (*Revelation of the Mystery*): "Knowledge of Him is attained only by unceasing bewilderment of the reason, and His favor is not procured by any act of human acquisition but is miraculously revealed to men's hearts."

DHAT: THE GROUND OF ALL BEING

Still, to pursue our investigation: what is Dhat? Dhat is the undifferentiated, uncreated, solitary place, the unique, precreation state of God, from which all being issues. Sufi metaphysicians believe that at the moment God made the decision to manifest, to express His or Her love of possibility, Dhat contracted, and part of its essence coalesced into *Nur*, or the light of creation—the all-pervading light of the physical universe and one of the Ninety-Nine Names of God.

Abdul Aziz Said, professor in the School of International Service at American University, Washington, D.C., and a Sufi sheikh, describes the state of Dhat this way (as paraphrased):

Imagine you are deep in the desert. It is late at night. You are far from civilization, far from any source of artificial illumination. The sky is overcast; there is no moon and the light of the stars is not visible. It is as dark as a coal mine two miles beneath the surface of the earth.

Within this darkness, you have made a campfire. The campfire gives off a flickering light. Imagine this campfire, and the light it gives off for as far into the wilderness as it can penetrate, is all of the universes, all creation, all the created planes of existence.

Dhat is all that is beyond this circle of light. It is the unchanging essence that creates and yet is unaffected by creation. It is the endless darkness beyond the campfire's light that has given birth to the campfire.

This place, this Dhat, is also the "solitude of peace" that Pir Vilayat Inayat Khan refers to in the quotation at the beginning of this chapter.

How do we know that Dhat is as I have described it? Beats me! Some of the great Sufi sages seem to have directly experienced Dhat. Nevertheless, Dhat is, as Al-Hujwiri so eloquently states, quite beyond the reach of human reason.

OUT OF *NUR*:
THE NINETY-NINE NAMES OF GOD

When Dhat contracted and creation came into existence, a variety of attributes formed within Nur, or the uncreated, all-pervading light of the cosmos. Two of them were the all-important states of Wahid, Multiplicity in Unity, and Ahad, Unity in Multiplicity, which I have already mentioned. The attributes in general, or Sifat, are the Ninety-Nine Names of God; the names are exports from Islam. Over the centuries, Sufism has adapted many of the Names as spiritual practices, among which are Nur, Quddus (Spirit), Wadood (Love), and *Adr* (Power). Another name for the collectivity of Attributes, along with Sifat, is *Wazaif*.

Pir Vilayat has explained that in Ahad—Unity in Multiplicity—all things, including energies and bodies both, form a single energy field, one without boundaries and one that pulsates within Dhat.

Wahid, Multiplicity in Unity, on the other hand, consists of an infinity of discrete entities. It is the expression of the trillions upon trillions of dust motes that make up individuated consciousnesses and all other separate entities in the universe—chairs, tables, elements, planets, stars, and so on and so forth.

The knight is privy to the consciousness of unity.

Therefore, he can fearlessly carry out actions within the multiplicity.

Was the Sufi warrior Shamyl in this state? Perhaps. It seems that the one and the many lie in a state of equanimity within the knight.

While the knight is not a member of an elite, he represents an unusually high degree of honor. His honor has to do with the Self and not the personality.

Hazrat Inayat Khan writes, "For a Sufi the sense of honor is not for his personality, he does not give his person a greater place than dust, and the central theme of his life is simplicity and his moral is humility. Yet remember that the Sufi breathes the breath of God, so he is conscious of the honor of God. His pride is greater, therefore, than the pride of every man. It is in the intoxication of this pride that he proves to be God-conscious."

I cannot define the God-consciousness of the Sufi warrior-priest for you. But I can give you exercises that will help you find it within yourself.

Exercise 16: Imagining the Knight

In this exercise, a mental picture is to be created from your imagination and from everything you have ever heard or read about a knight.

To do this, reach as far inside yourself as you can. Do not worry about whether the image is historically correct. Shamyl is an example of the warrior-knight. But you might just as well choose the Samurai warrior-knights of ancient Japan. Accounts tell us that the Samurai warrior is totally still and completely at peace—until the moment of conflict comes, when he is transformed into total action.

For this exercise, you need to conjure up in your mind not living, breathing human beings, but states that are images of the ideal. Try to imagine what these states are like, even though you can never live up to these ideals because they are just that, ideals. The image you conjure up may be far from the truth. But the point is not to conjure up an exact replica of reality. The point is to actually participate, to the extent that it is possible for you, in the experience of knighthood—not just look on. When you have sifted through some of these images and begun to grasp their essence, it might help you to imagine, if only for a moment, that you are fearless. Imagine this for the purposes of this exercise only! If you owe the Mafia $10,000 and it is threatening to break your legs, you are not going to be able to solve that problem simply by imagining that you are fearless. This exercise is not meant to help you solve the ordinary problems of your everyday life. No; I am simply asking you to try for a moment to feel what it would be like to be fearless. Can you do so with passion? If you can—good!

Now, try to imagine that God is being fearless through you. If you had rather not try this, at least try to imagine you are in a state of fearlessness, and while it is you who are the fearless one, that fearlessness is also the fearlessness of God being manifested through you. Remember that the knight participates in the divine attributes of Wahid—Multiplicity in Unity—and Ahad—Unity in Multiplicity. Try to imagine these two attributes of the divine as manifesting through you.

Now try to imagine that what the Sufis call *Qahr*—Divine Sovereignty—is manifesting in you. What would it feel like to have personal access in your being to this quality? I am not telling you that you do indeed have personal access to this quality; I am asking you to try to feel what it would be like to have that personal access.

A key ingredient in the successful carrying out of these exercises is what Pir-o-Murshid called "the art of repose." The art of repose is one of the keys to God-realization. It is remarkably difficult for all of us to relax, to be in that state of total relaxation in which none of our muscles is tense and our mind and emotions are on standby, simply doing nothing. That is the place you have to be in to know the mind of the knight, of the warrior-priest.

Exercise 17: The Art of Repose

Practice relaxation for the next two or three days. Let go of any preconceptions you may have about what constitutes the spiritual life. Let go of any notion you may have that a spiritual person is superior or the member of an elite. Slip back into the arms of the Trusted One—Him or Her whom I have been calling the Beloved—and simply empty your mind. See what comes. Let what comes, come, remembering to let go of all your presuppositions about what is to come. Maybe nothing will come. In which case, that is what comes. In that case, nothing is good.

When he concluded his public sessions, Pir Vilayat was in the habit of asking us to get down on one knee, as if we were medieval knights in a sacred sanctuary vowing allegiance to a sovereign. Pir Vilayat asked us to think, "I will," and to repeat *Fatah*—"the Opener"—several times while doing this. Fatah is that one of the Ninety-nine Names of God that refers to the opening of the heart—the outward expansion of our being in the service and devotion of God that Sufism calls for. Fatah is also used as an affirmation of other spiritual vows; it is not uncommon to recite it thirty-three times at the end of a personal retreat. Have you been able to slip back into the arms of the Trusted One and empty your mind a little? If so, try to stretch yourself a little bit more by imagining what it would be like not to have to think about doing this at all, but just to be it. Begin to imagine that state now, because it will take you a very long time to be able to realize it.

When I started out as a carpenter, too many years ago, the man I was working for told me it would take me two years to learn to use a hammer. I did not believe him. After all, the hammer is a simple tool, right? Two years later, almost to the day, I suddenly realized I was fastening two-by-fours together without thinking about the hammer. I was just doing it. But it had taken me the whole two years. You must never come to think, in pursuing the spiritual path, that there are things that simply cannot be done at all. The incorrect personal belief that something cannot be done is the first and greatest barrier to Self-realization. Get over that, and get back to doing your practice; there will come a day when the doing of it is so automatic that all you need to do is just be. Begin now to practice having access to the archetype of the knight; once you have acquired that access, it will come in very handy.

As Pir Vilayat said, "I can see God fragmenting Him/Herself, descending from the solitude of Unity, out of love for the possibility of me and of you, of the stars and of the atoms." The word *fragmenting* is key here. Within the blazing uncreated light of pure love, something was missing—or maybe nothing was missing and creation just happened, or maybe it just seemed like a good idea at the time, or maybe something else entirely was involved. The point is that it happened, and here we are, the results of that fragmentation, trying to attain once more to that uncreated light we dimly sense but of whose nature we are not at all sure. But we struggle on, because Sufism tells us, in its very subtle way, that what we suppose to be real is not real at all, and that what is truly real is hidden from us, veiled. We are also told that beneath the veils, inside the hidden rooms, there is a state of light-filled ecstasy that has created out of itself a new being—you!—and knows its power and its purpose, which you, being part of it, can know as well.

Sound good? How do you get some? Rumi provides a clue: "Remember the deep root of your being, the presence of your lord. Give your life to the one who already owns your breath and your moments. If you don't, you will be exactly like the man who takes a precious dagger and hammers it into his kitchen wall for a peg to hold his dipper gourd. You'll be wasting valuable keenness and foolishly ignoring your dignity and your purpose."

Exercise 18: You Are a Being of Light (II)

Imagine that you are a being of light, much greater than your physical body, expanding on the out-breath as far as you can imagine and contracting on the in-breath to just beyond the limits of your physical body. Keep this practice simple, and if you are able to keep your imagination focused for that length of time, do it for at least five minutes. What I mean by keep it simple is that if any other phenomena, such as lights or sounds, intrude, stop and start over again.

Our personalities are convinced that they are isolated. It does not seem to matter how many extraordinary experiences we have had; there is still a part of us—the larger part, most likely—that experiences itself as isolated and alone. It is not until we actually begin to experience the reality of our beingness as light that we become less burdened by this feeling of loneliness—which unfortunately does not mean that our personality automatically lets go of its negative commentaries. The personality needs to be prodded, it needs to be persuaded and stroked, before it will allow itself to be changed.

It is well and proper to ask your spiritual guide for advice about all the above. We have been talking about the knight of light, and, after all, in the age of chivalry it was the more experienced knights who took on and trained the less experienced knights, if only as role models. In Sufism as in similar spiritual pursuits, the more experienced guide takes on and trains the less experienced student. The person with the greater access to the capability of knighthood offers that access to the student/guidee.

Ultimately, of course, our loyalty, trust, and service are to be offered to God. I am not speaking here about blind faith, the robotic acceptance of whatever we fearfully think must be the Will of God. Those who know their duty, their purpose, their place, are also aware of their whole being; they know that they cocreate with the entire universe. It is, to say the least, empowering to know this; suddenly, you are bigger. Stay with that bigness. Become the knight of illumination that you are.

"What sense is there, O moth, in burning yourself in trying
to kiss the light?"
"My joy in it is greater than my sacrifice."
—Hazrat Inayat Khan

14

SACRIFICE

There is a branch of the Sufi Order called Ziraat, *ziraat* being the Farsi (Persian or Iraqi) word for farming or agriculture. In the Ziraat Order, *ziraat* means "spiritual farming."

Spiritual farming is the same as earthly agriculture in that in spiritual farming, you also have to plow up the ground before you plant again. And, just like real farming, everything has to be plowed up, every bit of old growth, even if it looks like it might still have some value. It all has to be discarded so that new growth—the growth of the spirit—can take place.

When we pursue the spiritual path and discover that old growth has to be discarded, we find that scary. Maybe we will have to sacrifice something we love!

It was not until I suddenly had a spate of apprehensive queries that I realized how great a worry this was for my students. One person was afraid she might have to give up her acting career. Another was worried she would lose the desire to create that was turning her into an accomplished woodworker. And so on.

And it is a concern. But when the process begins, you may find yourself sacrificing something you think you love and discovering that what you are sacrificing is not what you thought it was at all.

It happened to me. At the beginning of my spiritual career, I abruptly gave up something I dearly loved—or thought I did.

I am a competent chess player, certainly not world class, but above the level of the average wood-pusher. One afternoon in the early days of my stay at the Khanaqa as-Safiya in New York, I was sitting in the lounge playing a game of chess with a fellow Sufi student when the director walked by. As she passed us she glanced down at our chess board and muttered a single word. It sounded like "competition."

That word—or what I thought was that word—galvanized me into immediate action. From that moment on, I could not play chess any more. I swiftly gave away all my chess books. While doing this, I realized it was not chess I was sacrificing but my need to be successfully competitive. It was this need that had kept me at the game and made me think I enjoyed chess much more than I did.

But now, somehow, I did not need to compete successfully any more. So I did not sacrifice chess (in which I quickly lost interest); I sacrificed my need to compete successfully. I have noticed that people who have been on the spiritual path for some time rarely have hobbies or obsessive pastimes. They usually are not sports fans or collectors. They do have lives that they consider to be important—but there is not too much pastime clutter in those lives.

THE LAST CLASS

Sometimes you will find yourself compelled to give up something you did not particularly like in the first place but that for practical reasons you felt you could not give up. I had an older student who taught English composition and English literature for many years, sometimes full time, sometimes part time, here, there, and everywhere. He never liked teaching and did it to support his family. (He was engaged in other pursuits as well, such as writing, which are notorious for their inability to bring in much money.) Though he had this aversion to teaching, my student had always been successful and popular as a teacher.

But he set out along the Sufi path, almost offhandedly (he had not meant to take it seriously)—and then, one night, a month into the term, he stood in front of a classroom of students in a small university and could not think of a single thing to say. He canceled the class. The same thing happened in the next class—and the next. The next week, he resigned. He never returned to teaching.

This was not a wonderful experience for him. He was greatly distressed. It was not until a month after he had quit teaching that he realized what had happened (or began to realize; it would be some time before this would become his abiding belief): his steadily shifting inner Self could not fake teaching anymore; it had compelled him to be true, or truer, to who he really was.

Shifts in perception can emerge in unexpected and impractical ways. It is too easy to fool ourselves about these things. Sufism is a subtle process—sometimes almost a dangerous process—and in cases such as that of my student/English professor, it is best to consult a spiritual guide.

SELF-CHANGE AND RELATIONSHIP CHANGE

When you embark on the spiritual path, one of the things that seems to get sacrificed early on is the relationships you have accumulated to support whatever odd assumptions you have had about yourself. I mentioned earlier that your friends are going to be disturbed when they discover you are fooling around with your basic assumptions and reconsidering how you fit into the world. It can be very upsetting to those who are used to your being a certain way to see you expand, become softer, become more flexible; they will do their best to get you back to where you were before you got into this nonsense. This can become a serious struggle—especially because, at first, you and your friends will not necessarily understand what is happening.

Let's suppose that before you entered on the spiritual path, a significant portion of your creative energy went into talking about baseball. You and your friends argued statistics and the merits of players. Your emotions were bound up with the fortunes of a particular team.

Then you found meditation. That led to certain discoveries about yourself, and baseball began to seem trivial in comparison.

There is no way this will not upset your friends, who depend on you to talk baseball with them. The layer of humanity to which you were attached no longer works for you. To extricate yourself from this layer is going to be a delicate business. You may have to continue to pretend interest for some time while weaning your friends from your presence. All this becomes especially problematical when the friend in question is your spouse.

The changes in you, the shifts that take place, are very gradual. To the person in whom they are taking place—yourself—they seem colossal. You might tend to exaggerate them in your relations with your spouse in particular. Even when you do not exaggerate changes, your spouse may have trouble accepting them. Then you need to be as honest with your partner as you can be. Tell your spouse or significant other you have to do this spiritual work, and you would be very happy if he or she would simply support you. You are not asking your partner to participate; you are just asking him or her to be patient.

When your spouse, however unconsciously, tries to slow your progress, you will have to be patient yourself. This often happens. The slowing down of your progress can take the form of a variety of subtle undermining moves. Your spouse may even believe he or she is being supportive in making these moves.

Then again, you may be in for a big surprise. You may discover that your spouse or significant other or long-time companion is quite willing to support you.

I have seen both happen. Whether it is the one or the other does not seem to depend on any single factor, except perhaps the depth of self-confidence of the partner. The point is that when shifting from one layer of relationship to another—especially when you are in a marriage—abuses can take place, and we have to think carefully about what we are willing to sacrifice in the name of the greater good. My advice has always been that unless abuse of some sort is taking place, there is always a way to sort things out.

Perhaps it is not correct to speak of a shift from one layer of relationship to another. Perhaps it is more accurate to say that we acquire a broader view of reality, that our perception of reality is expanded. And when this begins to happen, it can really be quite devastating. We seem to be losing friends one after the other. To compound our anxieties, we often have no idea what is going on.

THE PRESENCE OF GRACE

While this experience of expansion may seem devastating (e.g., as regards losing old friends—though you will gain new ones), it is something that we on the spiritual path call grace.

What is grace? I suppose it can be seen as divine intervention in our personal affairs—God, sitting on his throne, occasionally (and, often it seems, all too arbitrarily) bestowing wisdom on random innocents. Or we can regard it as the doings of a sort of Grace Angel, whose only responsibility is to be on the lookout for likely candidates for grace. Another way to look at it is that somehow, from somewhere, a new dispensation comes upon us that was not previously available, and suddenly we know something we did not know before—or we feel a type of energy or emotion that was previously denied us, intense love for humanity, for example. It is certainly described often enough in the literature in the latter terms.

Perhaps all these definitions are true to one degree or another.

But I would rather put it this way: Since it is a basic tenet of Sufism that we are all a part of the being of God, then everything we do is also a part of that God. Thus in doing what we do, we respond to an activity of the divine; we function in our capacity as a part of the divinity and create a reality that, in our own seemingly limited sphere, is appropriate to the divine purpose.

What I am saying is that we are the purpose. Sufism also holds that all that exists is within us and is gradually unveiled; we already have the totality of revealed knowledge within us, but it is veiled from our consciousness. It has to be veiled; otherwise, it would interfere with our learning about physicalness. That, at least, is the theory. To the extent that we are determined to learn about it, more and more of this knowledge is revealed to us in living. The spiritual work we do is very much a part of this process. When we look at that work in this light, the sacrifices we make take on an entirely different aspect: they become a means to the lifting of the veil. There is a tension in all of us between what we want to do and the forces of society (including those we long ago interiorized) that are amassed against us. The power of these forces is often such that we do not even know what we want to do. But it is out of this tension that our personal power is forged. That forging depends upon how courageous we are about taking on these shifts in perception. If our commitment to illusion has been great, accepting these shifts can often seem very much like a sacrifice.

Rarely do people plunge willy-nilly, eagerly, into shifting from one level of experience to another. In fact, we in Sufism do not encourage such plunges. It is more common for people responding to the inner call to be timid in their actions, because they instinctively know that something big is about to happen, and they do not want to approach something big recklessly. (Besides, they say to themselves, this seeming shift may be some sort of a con, and—as Pir Vilayat used to say—sacrificing your life savings for a con is silly. "Don't quit your job!" the Pir meant. Caution is never unreasonable.) What many of us think of as "divine dispensation"—the seeming sudden miraculous intervention of God, a Guardian Angel, or whatever—is really, to the Sufi way of seeing things, a continuous, never-ending showering of the universe with compassion, mercy, spirit, peace, justice—all of it. At a certain point, an internal switch in us is tripped, and we begin to perceive and respond to this showering (perception and response being actually one and the same). The event may seem dramatic; and, after all, we all love a drama. But human beings also love—and insist upon—predictability. So when the divine dispensation—which was always there—comes upon us suddenly and unpredictably, we regard this spiritual windfall as an imposition, as a sacrifice.

But this new dispensation, this new wave of knowledge, of love, of joy, of whatever, however it manifests itself, demands a new response from us, and we are free to accept or reject this demand. At the same time, we generate the old responses, because that is what we are used to doing. The act of loving others, to cite but one example, can suddenly become a source of confusion, especially if we have always been selfish and demanding in our expression of what we think is love. Joy can be an even greater source of confusion if our experience of the world up until then has been mainly one of depression.

Joy Is Real, and Depression Is Not Inevitable

Depression is not inevitable. When people tell me they are depressed, I ask them what it feels like. Then I ask them what it feels like when they are not depressed. Usually, they cannot remember. But if they are caught off guard, people who are clinically depressed can sometimes throw off their depression, at least temporarily. I have seen this happen, sometimes in the middle of Sufi dancing: then, some of the worst depressives are capable of suddenly becoming responsive, expressive, joyful. Unfortunately, when the dancing stops, they remember they are depressed. It is as if they deliberately regather a black cloud around themselves. They resume calling the state of darkness in which they live "the world."

I know depression can be difficult. I have been there myself. What brought me out of my depression—and this is the key to getting out of depression—was deciding that the moments of joy we feel are real in themselves and not an escape from reality. It took me years and the sacrifice of what I considered a state of some profundity; which was really just a defense mechanism, to emerge from depression. Now I know it can be done just by deciding you are tired of feeling bad. The only things you need sacrifice are your wrong assumptions about reality.

Certainly, chemical imbalance can play a role in depression. But if you have an insightful psychiatrist who successfully addresses this problem, then once you have gotten yourself to a place of balance with the help of drugs, you can begin to examine your assumptions. I am a firm believer in addressing the symptoms first, and then the causes. Pir-o-Murshid had a powerful saying we in the Order quote constantly, though we are careful about how and when we say it. The saying is, "Shatter your ideal on the rock of truth." Sacrifice indeed. What this statement means, at least in part, is that whatever you take to be real usually is not. Your belief in that reality will do for a time, but if you are paying attention, eventually it will have to give way to a profounder truth. Do not assume you are so cool that all your ideals have already been shattered on the rock of truth. Nobody is that cool. We all must create ideals; they are the standards, the emblems of greater perfection, toward which we strive. The guide/student relationship falls into this category of a created ideal, as do the fine details of your belief in God. Most of us assiduously avoid acting on Pir-o-Murshid's admonition to "shatter your ideal on the rock of truth." Perhaps it is not the sort of thing you can do in a deliberate way. How would you know if you had succeeded anyway? But it is certainly within the power of all of us to examine what we accept or believe and then to search for alternatives. The true shattering of an ideal is a matter of a deep, deep shift in knowledge. Otherwise, it will be nothing but mere intellectual wheel spinning.

Death is a bridge whereby the lover rejoins the Beloved.
                                        —Rabia

15

DEATH

I grew up in a Protestant Christian household—Lutheran, to be exact. In my personal opinion, this religion is the height of self-righteousness.

Death was held up to us Lutherans as the point at which you either sink into the nether regions or are rewarded with eternal bliss. Eternal bliss sounded extremely dull. Spending eternity singing boring Lutheran hymns in a monotone does not sound at all exciting to a young lad bursting with energy. In Lutheranism, eternal bliss is the carrot leading you to behave properly, while the stick is hell and damnation—really bad guys poking you with red-hot irons and generally delighting in your torment.

When I was still quite young, I figured that even boring hymns were better than getting poked with red-hot irons. But, as a teenager, I began to wonder if there was not a third alternative.

My disenchantment with Lutheranism began innocently enough. In most religions, a teenager is required to attend a course of study. I highly recommend this, even if the child is uninterested or even resentful at the time, because a course of religious study teaches a child to think in religious terms.

What is taught may be simplistic, but it is a useful experience that will be advantageous in later years, perhaps in surprising ways. Every Saturday morning, when I would much rather have been doing more interesting things, I was taken by my parents to the church and stuffed with Christian/Protestant/Lutheran propaganda. Believe it or not, at the time I enjoyed the experience, for the most part. I tend to accept whatever is unavoidable and do what I have to do to get through that experience.

So there I was, with a group of other youthful captives, being taught the Lutheran perspective on the experience of living. My move away from Christianity began during an innocent conversation we were having with our pastor about obligation. The pastor was explaining how important it is to seek salvation, and that if you are once exposed to the message of Christianity—specifically Lutheran Christianity—then you are under an obligation to follow this path; otherwise, eternal damnation will be your lot.

I asked the pastor: if a Hindu walks past a Christian storefront in India and notices the Christian display in the window, say a cross or an effigy of Christ or whatever, then moves on without thinking anything further of it, not for the rest of his life, is that Hindu then doomed to damnation? The pastor replied in the affirmative.

I said nothing, and pretended to accept what he had said. But in my innermost being, it struck me that this was the dumbest thing I had ever heard the pastor say. It was the beginning of the end of my being a Lutheran.

I discovered later that most, if not all, religious denominations are so steeped in doctrine that they have completely lost sight of the message of Christ that animated them in the first place. I suppose every institution eventually loses touch with the essence of what formed it. At the time when I first got upset with my pastor, I could not separate doctrine from essence. What really bothered me was that that perfectly innocent Hindu, along with all the other innocent people who walked past that Christian storefront, were being condemned to an eternity of damnation without knowing it by a Lutheran pastor they had never met and never even heard of. It seemed so blatantly silly that I was confused about it for years.

Death in the East and West

Sufis have very clear and definite ideas about death. They regard it as nothing more than a door through which everyone must pass.

Hazrat Inayat Khan writes: "Death takes away the weariness of life, and the soul begins life anew. Death is a sleep from which the soul awakens in the hereafter. Death is the crucifixion after which follows the resurrection. Death is the night after which the day begins. It is death which dies, not life."

When you are young—unless you have directly experienced the death of someone close to you—death is an abstraction. It has no relation to your life. This is especially true in the Western world, where the cessation of the functioning of a human body is regarded simply as something that must be dealt with in the most sanitary way possible. We have created whole institutions around the avoidance of looking at death directly. Throughout most of history, when someone died, the family prepared the body for burial or interment, washed, wrapped in cloths or clothed in finery, and then burned or lowered into the ground. Now, when a body dies, it is efficiently whisked away by burial professionals, who gently direct the relatives' every move while making reassuring noises.

Hazrat Inayat Khan writes:

We will not be afraid of death once we have discovered the true
nature of the self. Once man has experienced the inner life, the
fear of death has expired; because he knows death comes to the
body, not to his inner being. When once he begins to realize
life in his heart and in his soul, then he looks upon his body as
a coat. If the coat is old he puts it away and takes a new one,
for his being does not depend upon his coat. The fear of death
lasts only so long as man has not realized that his real being
does not depend upon his body.

As a minister of the Sufi Order who is sometimes called upon to
officiate at funerals, I have been able to observe the efficiency of
burial professionals. Standing there in the funeral home, I am
all too aware that this is a business, and dealing efficiently with
the family is part of the business. I am also aware that even as
the body of the dead person is lying there looking perfect, the
soul of that person is hanging around trying to figure out what
is going on. All too often, I have had the experience of sitting in
the mortuary, waiting for the moment when the service begins,
and sensing the dead person's soul in a state of confusion over
what is going on. The people at the service are confused about
all this, too—which further confuses the soul. In focusing on
making the whole process of death and burial merely sanitary,
we have prevented ourselves from seeing what really happens
at a funeral.

We Americans no longer have any certainty regarding the
assumptions our culture once held about death. We may subscribe to a certain attitude due to our loyalty to a certain religion, but we cannot help being aware that there are other ways
of looking at death and dying today. As our absolute certainty

has slipped away, we have tended to substitute a sort of determined, stubborn mindset. What we see today is people sitting in a mortuary, paying their respects, as it were—except for the family, which is basically stuck there—while everybody is wondering what, if anything, is actually happening to the soul of the deceased. I am convinced much of the emotional turmoil flying about at a wake or funeral is due to the very natural worry this situation provokes in many of us about the nature and outcome of our own death. You cannot help noticing that your friend or relative is lying very still and will no longer be around to bother you or delight you. You cannot help asking yourself, "So what's going to happen to me?"

Confusing us further about death is the direct or indirect experience of violent death that we all are increasingly experiencing in the world today. We are more and more aware that people are being gunned down or in some manner killed, aimlessly or otherwise, at every moment of the day. We realize it could happen to us. We even realize that, practically speaking, we could fairly easily be at the other end of the gun ourselves. A Romanian friend of mine once told me that during her country's transition from Communism, she and a friend were walking down a street in Bucharest when her friend was casually shot down and killed by a sniper. There was no reason for this; it was offhand sniping taking place in the unrest of a transition period, people killing people just because they knew they could get away with it. You can imagine how deeply affected my friend was by this. The experience persuaded her to find a way to come to the United States, where she thought she would be safe. Everywhere in the world today, the increasing presence of random, violent death makes us all the more confused about the nature of death.

Death in Life

There are those, however, for whom the limited explanations of the world are never enough, for whom death will always remain truly a puzzle. These people really want to know exactly what death is. Is it a total extinguishing? Is there a beyond, and if so, what is its nature?

There is only one way to know this, short of actually dying, and that is to go within. Have you noticed how eagerly many of us latch onto stories of near-death experiences? Such experiences happen within—that is, within the consciousness of the person who has seemingly died. The experience is being thought or dreamed; it is not an external one but an internal one. Those who have near-death experiences see a tunnel or a white light, but their eyes are closed; they are unconscious, but they still touch or feel those who approach them. How do they manage this? Not with their physical senses. But they still use the body as a reference point. Perhaps this is not really necessary, but they have been so used to the reality of their bodies, that reality is still so compelling, that they cannot ignore it.

In the course of near-death experiences, the experiencers meet their previously departed Mom or Dad or Uncle Albert, or perhaps a religious figure they are attached to; they converse with these entities and then return to their earthly bodies to do additional work. This is not an experience you deliberately want to have, but we still sometimes do envy persons who have had it. They have experienced a reality that we are only told exists, and they have come back with a certainty that those of us who are more material minded and matter-of-fact can never have. Sometimes, we envy that certainty.

The question is: how can we—without dying!—acquire that degree of certainty?

Pir Vilayat was always extremely reluctant to talk about death, but when the subject came up, he would occasionally refer to his astral travels as proof for him of life beyond life. He was reluctant to talk about this, because he did not want people to think that only through astral traveling, which not everybody can readily do, could proof of the existence of an afterlife be obtained. He did not want people concentrating on astral travel to the exclusion of other practices. And in this he was correct.

We do not need to astral travel to obtain knowledge of life after death.

There is a condition that the initiate can achieve that is fairly commonly taught in the various esoteric schools. It takes a lot of work to achieve this state, but the upshot is that you arrive in a place where the body is no longer important and where you are adrift in a kind of cosmic sea of love or peace or serenity. Thinking is different there, because you are not limited by your synaptic impulses. In this state it is not uncommon to think of your body simply as a conveyance you get in and out of, or a suit of clothes you put on and take off. I guess that until you have actually experienced it, you will have to take the existence of this state on faith—but it is there to learn about, and the path is well trodden.

Hazrat Inayat Khan writes, "Verily, the soul has no birth, no death, no beginning, no end. Sin cannot touch it, nor can virtue exalt it; it has always been and always will be, and all else is its cover like a globe over the light."

THE PASSING OF MICHAEL

I have already spoken about my friend Michael Qayoom Brain, a member of our Sufi Order who became terribly ill with stomach cancer. I have talked about how he rallied and fought and lived on for many more months than the doctors had initially expected.

On April 2, 1999, a little before noon, Michael made his transition to the next phase of existence. He had had a very difficult year, not only because of the chemotherapy, but also because his cancer was in his intestines and stomach and for much of the time this prevented him from eating. Nevertheless, Michael used his time well. My experience with him over the last year of his life was that of an observer privileged to partially experience someone else's transformation. At the very end, in the last week, it occurred to me that over the past year Michael had gone through all the stages of a spiritual retreat, very slowly and with great intensity. At one point, I asked him where he was—I meant spiritually—and he replied that he was "just above Hobbitville" and wanted to know where that was. I told him he was probably in what we Sufis call *Mithal*, a new level of consciousness, emerging as a sort of rebirth, that corresponds to the realm of metaphor and image in which thoughts become translated into forms. Michael liked the idea. He did not know about such things as Mithal because he had always avoided the formal retreat process. During his last retreat he had ignored the practices and spent the entire six days drawing—and that retreat had been ten years before. The nature of Michael's life was such that he was in a retreat space most of the time, and probably did not need the formal process. In the last year of his life, he felt that knowing when he was going to die was a great gift; it focused his attention remarkably. When I look back on it, I can see him going through each stage of a one-year retreat: pondering it; worrying about it; making sure he thoroughly knew the stage he was in before moving on to the next. I am not sure he was necessarily aware of this process, because it took place over so long a period of time—but I do think that, at some level, he knew exactly what he was doing.

The soul is so much larger than our petty notions about it! Toward the end, in his room, those of us who were privileged to visit Michael did not talk much; talking was too fatiguing for him. What we found ourselves doing—we had not planned this beforehand at all; it just happened—was the practice of saying Dhikr (the Remembrance of God) on the breath (that is, silently), each according to his own rhythm. Michael did not; mostly he slept. And as we did Dhikr, I noticed that the rhythms of our breath seemed to fall together. There we were, Michael's wife, Sharifa, Majida, and me, doing Dhikr on the breath and having an experience of peace and joy and hope and reassurance. We did not talk about this until after Michael had passed away; somehow it was just too precious an experience to talk about.

Finally, on Friday, April 2, 1999, the hospice nurse telephoned to tell me Michael's time had come. I dropped what I was doing and drove straight to the hospital. I found Sharifa sitting in the darkened room holding Michael's inanimate hand; Michael had passed away, and Sharifa was sitting there with a look very much like bliss on her face. As soon as she saw me the tears came, and I remember the electricity that passed between us as I reached down to kiss her on the cheek and our tears mingled. I can still feel that sensation. I forced myself to look at the still form lying on the bed that had once partially contained my friend Michael. I was almost moved to straighten his hair. But I did not; instead, I sat down.

That was when I noticed the particular atmosphere in the room. It was as if the heavens had opened and all the great beings of the spiritual hierarchy had come down and were much closer—or maybe they had always been close, and we were just much more sensitive to them now. I was very aware of Michael's joyful presence. I had a sense that he had moved on, that he had returned home—and suddenly I wondered why we were crying.

It was then that Sharifa told me that when she had seen Michael the previous evening, for the last time before he had lost consciousness forever, his first words to her as she walked into his room had been, "Good-bye. I have work to do." At the time Sharifa was taken aback by this. But now she understood what Michael had meant, and a feeling almost of gratitude was mingled with her feelings of grief.

In a way, I almost envied Michael. He had gotten to find out about—to dwell in—a reality that those of us who have to carry on down here for a little while longer can only visit in bits and pieces. Since Michael's passing, I have asked myself why I felt so little grief; he was, after all, one of my closest friends of the last twenty years. I asked Sharifa about this (she had felt the same way), and we decided that we had not grieved more at Michael's death because we saw no point in grieving deeply; we knew what had really happened to him and where he had really gone. Of course, we felt sad—she more than I, of course—but there was no longer any need to loudly professes our grief. We had spent our time grieving at the beginning of the illness—and then Michael had begun to show us how truly to implement the teachings of Sufism. Now he is having a good time, and we are still down here slogging away. I guess we should all start having a good time too.

Death takes away the weariness of life,
and the soul begins life anew.
Death is a sleep from which the soul awakens in the hereafter.
Death is the crucifixion after which follows the resurrection.
Death is the night after which the day begins.
It is death which dies, not life.

—Hazrat Inayat Khan

16

So What Do
I Do Now?

A friend read the manuscript of this book and inquired, "You aren't going to just stop there, are you?" When I asked her what more she wanted, she replied, "Well, I want to know what to do next. After I'm finished reading the book, then what?"

Good question. If only there were an easy answer. The truth is, spiritual literature tends to oversimplify. "Okay, reader," it implies, "just follow these four rules/these seven steps/these eleven principles outlined in the book. Illumination will then be yours. At the very least, you will become very happy and contented."

This is something that it is easy for the writer to say and that every reader wants to hear. But the truth is more complicated. The fact is, each of us is a work in process. We are compilations of what we have experienced thus far and suggestions of what we may experience in the future. On the other hand, as Abi-Ru says in the foreword, anything we read can only set us searching, not end the search. Words are static. Spiritual evolution is dynamic. What you read here may help you begin the quest, but it is not intended to walk you to your journey's end.

One of the most important Sufi thoughts is that each person is unique—not just in a murky "let's celebrate diversity" way, but truly and amazingly a unique manifestation of the One. Each path is an individual path; each spiritual journey is singular and distinct from every other. Tempting as it is to lay down universal laws and commandments, Sufis resist that temptation. The great Persian Sufi poet Sa'adi wrote, "Every soul is born for a certain purpose, and the light of that purpose is kindled in his soul."

So, as a Sufi, I am reluctant to tell you what your own next step should be. On the other hand, I do like to talk. So I do not mind joining you in some speculation about what that next step might be.

Keep reading, for a start. If you have discovered that you are interested in the Sufi Path, you are in luck—there are Sufi writings enough to fill a library. There are so many translations of Rumi, for instance, that you can choose your favorite flavor. Read and think about what you have read.

Take a class. Start yoga. Practice meditation. Once you have stepped firmly on the spiritual path, you will be surprised how much company you have. Even if you are in a small town, explore the connections that you can make on the Internet. On page 209 I have listed a few Web sites to get you started. Do not rely just on those. Do your own research, and you will be amazed by how many searchers are out there. (It is not called the World Wide Web for nothing!)

Perhaps the most important clue I can offer about what to do next is this: trust yourself. As I said, it is your own individual path. Trust what you yourself feel is true about your experiences. Sure, we are all looking for validation. We want somebody—or everybody—to tell us, "Yes, that's genuine. Yes, that's a true spiritual experience. You're on the right track. Now you've got it!" It is natural to long for company and guidance and even approval. It is natural—but not necessary. After all, when we share spiritual experiences, we are just describing to one another our universe and all its possibilities and potentials.

Even those of us who are "spiritually advanced" can forget to trust ourselves. Majida, my wife, was practicing an advanced breathing technique with a teacher. Suddenly, Majida found herself in a place beyond thought. She came back confused and disoriented, unsure about what she was supposed to be doing. Convinced that she had failed to do the exercise correctly, she told the teacher about what had happened. "Consider yourself blessed," the teacher told her. "It's a very rare state, that intelligence without an object." Thinking about the teacher's words, Majida realized that she had attained similar states many times over the years—and then criticized herself for being loopy and forgetful. Hearing that this kind of consciousness was desirable opened her mind in a new way. Previously, she had not trusted her own experience.

Having finished this book, you may have the feeling that you are standing with your hand on the handle of a door still closed to you. You may want me to tell you to go ahead and open that door or be waiting for further instructions about which way the handle turns. But, you see, it is your door, your handle, your hand. Trust yourself. Trust your ability to learn. Trust the validity of your personal search. It is yours. When you are ready, look for your guide.

Until then, trust the guide within you.

WEB SITES

- Sufi Order in the West: <http://www.sufi.order.org>
- Web site created by Pir Vilayat distilling his teachings into a series of meditation exercises: <http://www.theuniversel. net>
- Complete works of Hazrat Inayat Khan: <http://www. wahiduddin.net>
- Books on Sufism and related topics: <www.omegapub. com>
- Sufi Order in Europe events: <http://www.zenithinstitute. com>
- Program founded by Pir Vilayat Inayat Khan designed to enable the poor to help themselves: <http://www. hopeprojectindia.org>

SELECTED
BIBLIOGRAPHY

Addas, C. *The Quest for Red Sulphur: The Life of Ibn 'Arabi*. Cambridge, U.K.: Islamic Texts Society, 1993.

Arasteh, R. *Growth to Selfhood: The Sufi Contribution*. London: Routledge and Kegan Paul, 1980.

———. *Rumi, the Persian: Rebirth in Creativity and Love*. Tucson, Ariz.: Omen, 1972.

Armstrong, Karen. *The Battle for God*. New York: Knopf, 2000.

———. *A Short History of Islam*. New York: Modern Library, 2000.

Bayat, M., and M. A. Jamnia. *Tales from the Land of the Sufis*. Boulder, Colo.: Shambhala, 1994.

Burke, O. M. *Among the Dervishes*. New York: Dutton, 1975.

Chittick, W. C. *The Sufi Path of Knowledge*. Albany: State Univ. of New York Press, 1989.

———. *The Sufi Path of Love: The Spiritual Teachings of Rumi*. Albany: State Univ. of New York Press, 1983.

al-Ghazzali. *The Alchemy of Happiness*. Translated by Claud Field. Lahore, Pakistan: Sh. Muhammed Ashraf, 1964.

Ibn 'Arabi, M. *The Bezels of Wisdom*. Translated by R. W. J. Austin. New York: Classics of Western Spirituality, 1980.

———. *What the Seeker Needs*. Translated by T. Bayrak and R. Harris. Putney, Vt.: Threshold, 1992.

Jami. *Yusuf and Zulaikha: An Allegorical Romance*. Edited, abridged, and translated by David Pendlebury. London: Octagon, 1980.

Kabir. *The Kabir Book: Forty-four of the Ecstatic Poems of Kabir*. Versions by Robert Bly. Boston: Beacon, 1977.

Khan, Hazrat Inayat. *Complete Works*. 14 vols. Geneva, Switzerland: Servire, 1980.

211

——. *The Heart of Sufism: An Anthology*. Edited by H. J. Witteveen. Boulder, Colo.: Shambhala, 1999.

——. *The Inner Life*. Lebanon, N.Y.: Omega, 1989.

——. *Spiritual Dimensions of Psychology (Collected Works)*. Lebanon, N.Y.: Omega, 1990.

Khan, Hidayat Inayat. *The Inner School: Esoteric Sufi Teachings*. Victoria, B.C., Canada: Ekstasis, 1997.

——. *Sufi Teachings: Lectures from Lake O'Hara*. Victoria, B.C., Canada: Ekstasis, 1996.

Khan, Vilayat Inayat. *Awakening: A Sufi Experience*. New York: Jeremy P. Tarcher/Putnam, 2000.

Moinuddin, Hakim. *The Book of Sufi Healing*. New York: Inner Traditions International, 1985.

Rumi, Mevlana Celaleddin. *Crazy As We Are*. Translated by N. Ergin. Prescott, Ariz.: Hohm, 1992.

——. *Rumi: Fragments, Ecstasies*. Translated by Daniel Liebert. Santa Fe, N.M.: Source Books, 1981.

——. *Say I Am You*. Translated by John Moyne and Coleman Barks. Athens, Ga.: Maypop, 1994.

Shafii, M. *Freedom from the Self: Sufism, Meditation and Psychotherapy*. New York: Human Sciences, 1985.

Shah, Idries. *Seeker After Truth*. London: Octagon, 1982.

——. *Tales of the Dervishes*. New York: Dutton, 1970.

——. *The Way of the Sufi*. New York: Dutton, 1970.

van Stolk, S., and Daphne Dunlop. *Memories of a Sufi Sage: Hazrat Inayat Khan*. London: East-West, 1990.

Vaughan-Lee, L. *Travelling the Path of Love*. Inverness, Calif.: Golden Sufi Center, 1995.

Vitray-Meyerovitch, Eva de. *Rumi and Sufism*. Translated by Simone Fattal. Sausalito, Calif.: Post-Apollo Press, 1987.

INDEX

INDEX

Shadhili, xi
Shahid, 46–47
Shamyl, 171, 172, 175
sheikh, 8, 32–33, 91, 110–12,
    171, 173
Shirzan, Abi-Ru, 203
Sifat, 165, 174
silsila, 112, xi
skydiving, 103–4
sophia, ix
Sorbonne, University of
    Paris, 6
soul
    death and, 195, 196, 197
    exaltation and, 153
    happiness and, 12–18
    Hazrat Inayat Khan on, 40,
        144, 153, 195, 199
    meditation and, 14
    Rumi on, 153
    Sa'adi on, 206
    sovereign, 124, 125
    spiritual yearning of, 146
soul-mate, 161–62
Sovereign of the Universe,
    64
Soviet empire, 172
spiritual(ity)
    creativity in, 122–25
    Eastern thoughts of, 153
    farming, 183
    path, 122–27, 128–31, 183–87,
        188–90, 206
    possessions and, 146–47
    responsibility and, 128–30
    vulnerability and, 161

yearning for the unattainable,
    145–46, 148–51, 152–56
Sufi Message, xi
Sufi Movement, 6
Sufi Order
    higher standards of, 63–65
    initiation into, 130
    leadership of, xii
    representatives of, 64
    Ziraat, 183
Sufi Order International, 5, 7,
    9, xi
Sufi Path. see also Sufi Way
    the call, 87–92, 206
    definitions of, x
    embarrassment and, 55–56,
        61–63
    of love and service, 92–93
    memory and, 85–87
    persistence and, 85
Sufi Way, 146, 189, x, xi. see also
    Sufi Path
Sufi(s), ix–x
Sufism
    being of light, 52
    embarrassment and, 55–65
    intentions and, 117–18
    isolation and, 77
    orders of, xi
    path of heart, 113–15
    process of, 185
    teacher and, 112
    tenets of, 188
    truth and, 49–50
Suhrawardi, 7
Suluk Academy, 7

218

surrender
addictions and, 71–72
beings of light and, 74–79
to Beloved, 67–68
definitions of, 67–68
exercises for, 73, 74–76
Hazrat Inayat Khan on, 66
Jelal, 73–74
Jemal, 73–74
Kemal, 73–74
Wahdat Al Wujud, 68–70
willing, 68
Yearning Switch and, 80–81

tasawwuf, xii
teacher; guide, 50–52, 88–94,
105, x–xi
Teresa of Avila, Saint, 41
Tijani, xi
time-space world, 100
transformation, 35, 84–85, 105,
163, 200, xi
trust, 159–64
Trusted One, 177, 178. see also
Beloved
truth, 49–51, 56–61, 191

unhappiness, 11–12, 21–23
Unicorn Phase, 88
Unity of Existence. see Wahdat
Al Wujud
Universal Mind, 84

Voltaire, 54
vow(s), 105, 107, 108
vulnerability, 159–64

Wadood, 164–65, 174
Wahdat Al Wujud, 11, 68–70, 97
Wahid, 172, 174, 176
warrior-knight, 172, 175
warrior-priests, 172, 175, 177
Wazaif, 174
Web sites, 206, 209
Will of God, 180

yearning for unattainable,
143–46, 148–51, 152–56
Yearning Switch, 80–81

Zat, 172
zikr, 116
Ziraat; ziraat, 183

ABOUT THE AUTHOR

Phillip Gowins was born in Minneapolis, Minnesota, in 1945. He has been a cabinetmaker since 1980. In 1979, he met Pir Vilayat Inayat Khan and shortly thereafter was inducted into the Sufi Order in the West. A teacher in that order, he lives in Scranton, Pennsylvania, with his wife, Dawn, who is also a teacher.

Phillip Gowins is available for workshops. To contact him, send an email to Phillip_Gowins@hotmail.com, or visit his blog at http://thesovereignsoul.blogspot.com/.

"Phillip Gowins's *Practical Sufism* is an amazing book that will assist readers to develop the highest form of values."

—Helen C. Donguines,
Assistant Dean of Instruction,
La Carlota City College, Phillippines

Quest Books

encourages open-minded inquiry into
world religions, philosophy, science, and the arts
in order to understand the wisdom of the ages,
respect the unity of all life, and help people explore
individual spiritual self-transformation.

Its publications are generously supported by
The Kern Foundation,
a trust committed to Theosophical education.

Quest Books is the imprint of
the Theosophical Publishing House,
a division of the Theosophical Society in America.
For information about programs, literature,
on-line study, membership benefits, and international centers,
see www.theosophical.org
or call 800-669-1571 or (outside the U.S.) 630-668-1571.

Related Quest Titles

The Heart of the Qur'an, by Lex Hixon
Heart, Self, and Soul, by Robert Frager
Perfume of the Desert, by Andrew Harvey

To order books or a complete Quest catalog,
call 800-669-9425 or (outside the U.S.) 630-665-0130.